WESTERN WINGS

WESTERN WINGS

Hunting Upland Birds on the High Plains

Ben O. Williams

WILLOW CREEK PRESS®

Published by Willow Creek Press, Inc.
P.O. Box 147, Minocqua, Wisconsin 54548

Printed in the United States

Dedication
This book is for Bobbie, who has always supported my hunting endeavors, who encouraged me to keep a kennel full of bird dogs, who takes care of them when I'm gone, and who pleasantly greets, feeds, and houses all the hungry hunting partners that I bring home.

Acknowledgments
I owe a special thanks to a host of friends and dogs who have hunted with me over the years.

TABLE OF CONTENTS

FOREWORD

Hunting birds on the High Plains, like living on the High Plains, requires a new handbook for conducting business. The situation is so unlike the eastern woodlands and the Midwestern farm fields that it's safest not to mention the two in the same breath.

Huns, sharptails, sage grouse, prairie chickens, pheasant, and mountain grouse all inhabit a country ruled—to the eye of the neophyte—by monotony. To the veteran sojourner, these lands reveal infinite refinement, richness, subtlety, and constant evolution. The western grasslands are a muted paradise equal in fascination to the more easily appreciated alpine landscapes that are often nearby.

I've known Ben Williams for thirty years and it is my impression that he has been afield the entire time I've known him. It is safe to say that his commitment is unparalleled. Before I read this book, I thought the commitment was to hunting. Now, I'm not so sure, though hunting is an undetachable part of it, as are the dogs, the enormous number of dogs that Ben has trained on wild birds in wild country. Ben no longer tells you how many birds he has shot, as he did when I first knew him; I'm not sure he wants it to get out how few he shoots. He is a hunter and he has dogs to break, but as I think the reader of this book will agree, Ben Williams has elevated his view until it encompasses the well-being of the birds and the lands he loves. This is the state at which the mature and highly evolved hunter finally arrives. Ben Williams has logged his many hours and miles like a diligent field biologist, and he has moved beyond hot barrels, empty shell casings, and game recipes to a wide, wide view in which the hunter, the land, and the quarry hold something eternal together.

—Thomas McGuane
McLeod, Montana

INTRODUCTION

I came to love and appreciate the prairie grasslands as a child. I was raised in northern Illinois; not knowing it was once the home of the tallgrass prairie and the greater pinnated grouse.

I lived on a twelve-acre farm, and a neighbor would plant corn in our field each spring. After planting, the field was never cared for, but it was good for wildlife. An old wooden fence surrounded the cornfield, which was overgrown with timothy, thistles, milkweed, and numerous other woody plants. It was a wonderful place for bobwhite quail to raise their families. Surrounding the small acreage were grain fields and pastures. Pheasants and rabbits lived along the untended spur line railroad tracks in the back of the field. The rails were only used two or three times a week. Maintenance was minimal; the tracks were overrun with chokecherry and hazelnut bushes along both sides.

During hunting season, my grandpa would ride his bicycle the eight miles from his place and spend several days with us. His beautiful silver bike had a wire basket and a mutton case strapped to the side, which held his Winchester '97 shotgun. When he arrived, he would place the bike on the front porch, chaining and locking it around one of the pillars. He'd carry in the mutton case and put it on the table in the vestibule.

Never one to hurry, Grandfather always waited for the weather to warm before going hunting each morning. He dressed in a wide-brimmed hat, a khaki shirt, and khaki riding breeches with leather leggings strapped over his boots up to his knees. He no longer kept hunting dogs, and I'm not sure to this day whether he wanted me, a young second-grader, to go along as a hunting companion or just a bird-dogger (someone to break brush so he could stay out in the open).

One day, he uncased the 12-gauge, put it together, and leaned it against the wall. He then put on his hunting coat and filled the loops with shells. I can still visualize the No. 6 on the tops of the paper shotgun shells. The gun slipped along the wall, and he reached out to stop it, asking me if I'd hold it. I liked that gun, with its bright blue shiny finish and dark walnut stock.

The shucked corn was already down when we walked along the edge of the field. He instructed me to do a little bird-dogging. I was thrilled and hopped over the wooden fence opposite him. I was small and couldn't walk fast, but he was old and did not walk fast, either. He pointed out quail droppings and feathers along the way.

At the railroad tracks, we heard a pheasant crow. The cover was heavy, but I made my way through. A covey of quail exploded beneath my feet. Three shots rang out. A bird dropped in the brush, one on the railroad tracks, and I thought I saw another drop on the other side of the tracks.

"You got three!" I yelled.

He picked up the bird on the tracks as I worked my way to the bird that dropped in the heavy cover. After spying a few feathers, I scooped it up.

"Grandpa," I said, "I think you shot a third bird that fell on the other side of the tracks."

"No, son, I don't think so."

I asked him if I could look and he replied, "Go ahead." I was sure he had shot the third bird. I looked a long time for that quail, but to no avail. Grandpa waited, and after a while he told me that it was no use.

We hunted another hour that day, then sat down to rest on an old log and looked at the beautiful birds. One was a hen, the other a cock.

Back at the house, he cleaned the birds and hung them by the silver bike.

I told my mother, "Grandpa got three quail."

He answered, "No, son, I only got two."

I helped him clean the Winchester '97. He showed me how to break it down and put it back in the mutton case. After supper, he lit his pipe and sat by the fire while he told me stories about shooting quail over pointing dogs. I thought to myself that having a bird dog to run through cover would be a lot easier.

Grandfather hunted the following day and shot a couple more quail and a pheasant. They were hanging above the bike when I got home from school that afternoon. I asked if he was going to hunt again the next day, and he said, "No, I have four quail and a pheasant. That's enough."

I was very young when my grandfather passed away. I don't remember any of the details. I just figured he was old. But what I do remember is that Grandfather was a gentleman hunter, and I live by that rule to this day.

GRAY PARTRIDGE
Rusty Tail, Rusty Gate

I was walking across a hay meadow in northern Illinois, training two young Brittanys. It was late September 1956—hot and dry for that time of year—and scenting conditions were poor. I crossed into a cornfield with the dogs working ahead of me and followed a long, grassy swale back toward the hunting rig. The grass was high, with walls of green corn eight feet high around me. The swale closed down into a marshy sliver with sedge spikes bursting in the sunlight. One dog slowed and half-pointed, unsure of himself, and the other young dog raced down alongside his partner and stopped. Both dogs raised their heads high, scented the air, moved off hesitantly down the narrow, silvery draw, and stopped again. I thought they had found several running pheasants and cautioned, "Easy now, whoa, easy."

Slowly they moved ahead and stopped. This time of year, long before hunting season begins, pheasants behave a lot better for pointing dogs. I rushed in to flush the birds before they had a chance to run into the corn.

There was an amazing whirl of wings and loud, harsh shrieks that sounded much like rusty gates swinging reluctantly open. The birds cleared the top of the corn tassels with rusty red tails visible. I was startled. I called the dogs back, not sure what I had seen—not bobwhites (too big), not pheasants (too small). I had heard about a covey bird called a partridge, but didn't think the birds were present in Illinois.

Later that day, I went to the college library and found what I was looking for in a North American gallinaceous bird book. It read: "European gray partridge, *Perdix perdix*, from central and southeastern Europe, introduced into the United States around the Great Lakes region in the early 1900s, larger than quail, has a reddish tail, very vocal and noisy taking off." That was my first encounter with a bird that I would come to know quite well in the decades ahead.

A few years later, I accepted a teaching position in central Washington. One day I was walking a large sagebrush flat along a small coulee, conditioning my dogs before hunting season, and looking for valley quail. The dogs pointed, and I walked in to flush the birds. This time, I knew they were gray partridge—also called Hungarian partridge or Huns—by the burst of whirling wings and loud, harsh shrieks. They flew off across the flat, and I watched them land again. I crossed the silver-blue sea of sagebrush to where I had marked them down. The dogs pointed, and the birds repeated their same noisy flight in tight formation. These wonderful covey birds intrigued me, and I wanted to learn more about them. I was hooked for life.

A couple of years later I moved on, not because the teaching salaries were higher, but because there was a place where the fishing and bird hunting were better and the prairies more open.

Since then, I have had thousands of encounters with pointing dogs and flushing grays. I may not get as startled as I did in my first encounter, but I still love the flush: the noisy burst, rusty tails, and harsh shrieks—the sound of a rusty gate.

ORIGINS

The natural range of the gray or Hungarian partridge included the eastern countries of Europe and central and southwestern Asia. The climate in that part of the world largely corresponds to the climate the partridge now occupies here in North America, with moderately cool to cold winters and heavy snow that covers the ground for only short periods of time due to frequent thaws and high winds. Many other factors influence where these birds can live. Various combinations of food, climate, weather, soil, cover, and topography have played an important part in their establishment and success in new regions, and the gray partridge is now one of the most widespread upland game birds in the world.

The partridge was first introduced into North America about the same time as the ring-necked pheasant, but early attempts failed. The dates of these early introductions are very sketchy due to poorly kept records, but it seems that the most successful stocking occurred in the early 1900s near Calgary, Alberta, Canada. After a few years the population exploded, with birds spreading to southern Alberta, Saskatchewan, and south into the United States. Minnesota, Montana, and other states also introduced Huns as early as the 1920s, although with limited success. Numerous introductions were made in other parts of North America through the early part of the twentieth century, but these largely failed as well. The major population of Huns now established in the northwestern and north-central states is believed to be descended from the Alberta stocking.

DISTRIBUTION

The largest distribution of Huns in the northwestern United States is from Lake Michigan west to the Columbia River in Washington. At one time, nineteen states had wild populations of Huns. Today, about sixteen states and three Canadian provinces claim established populations.

The highest density of Huns in the U.S. is in North Dakota, South Dakota, Montana, Idaho, Oregon, and Washington. Alberta and Saskatchewan lead in population density in Canada. The northern limits of the Canadian birds extend to the edges of boreal forest and aspen parklands, where agricultural land is present. Western populations occupy farmed and grassland valleys, but not forested areas.

The area that birds occupy today is probably the extent of their usable range.

KNOWING THE BIRD

The gray partridge (*Perdix perdix*), known throughout North America as the Hungarian partridge, or simply Hun, is an Old World bird. There are eight recognized subspecies in Europe, with a great variation in plumage, but these generally fall into two distinct groups: The eastern birds tend to be paler and grayer than their darker cousins of the west. Little information is known about the subspecies of North American populations, but most were derived from the Hungarian race in Europe.

The full-grown Hun is between the bobwhite quail and the

The Gray partridge known throughout North America as the Hun.

sharp-tailed grouse in size. The average weight of both sexes is twelve to fifteen ounces, and the total length of an adult is around twelve to fourteen inches, with a wingspan of fifteen to seventeen inches. The plumage of the sexes is similar; however, upon close examination there are obvious differences. In flight, the male and female are nearly impossible to tell apart. Most males have a well-developed, chestnut-brown horseshoe on their lower breast. But this can be a poor method of sex identification as some females share this distinctive trait. Furthermore, flushed birds usually fly away from the hunter, and the horseshoe is rarely visible. I once told one of my guests, a novice Hun hunter, that we could only shoot the males—the ones with the horseshoe. After my dogs made the first point of the day, I informed my guest that it is impossible to distinguish between the sexes in flight and to shoot away. To this day, I don't know whether the attempted horseshoe identification harmed his score.

At all ages, the male has only a single whitish-buff longitudinal stripe on each shoulder feather.

Later that day, we finally had a few birds in hand. I pulled a feather from the wing covert of one of the birds. It had a light buff longitudinal stripe down the center, identifying it as a cock. With the next bird I did the same; it had creamy crossbars running out from the central longitudinal stripe, marking it as a hen.

The partridge is a plump bird with short, rounded wings that include ten primaries and heavily mottled feathers. Diagonal chestnut-brown bands start under the wings and extend down and back on both sides to the belly. The cheeks and throat are gray. The bill, legs, and feet of the adults are bluish-white. It appears in flight as a grayish-brown bird without bright markings, but its short, round, rusty outer tail easily distinguishes it from other upland game birds.

Huns usually burst from cover straight into the air in a compact covey. Once airborne, these swift fliers utter a cackling, high-pitched *chrrk, chrrk, chrrk* that sounds much like a rusty gate being opened. Very quickly the covey can obtain speeds of over forty miles per hour. The birds are strong fliers, with quick, noisy wing beats for the first ten to thirty yards, followed by a glide that alternates with rapid wing beats until landing.

Huns differ considerably from other covey birds when flushed in that they usually fly in tight formation, close to the ground. If their flight path is unobstructed, they will usually follow a straight line over the nearest hill or highest landform. Once out of sight, the covey may hook right or left before alighting. If one or more hunters are positioned in the escape corridor, the flush will usually be higher in the air, and the covey will not be in compact formation. While the birds may break up and fly in many directions, they often regroup in flight so that they can stay in close proximity to their designated landing site.

One year, using pointing dogs late in the hunting season, I flushed the same covey eleven times, and they never did break up, even after shots were fired. This is not always the case; many times the covey will break up after three or four flushes and use different escape routes. When pursued, the covey will often fly back to the area where they were originally flushed or assemble close to a roosting site. Still, Huns are about as predictable as wind-driven snow. You never know exactly where they're going to settle.

Over the years, however, I have observed some patterns in their flight. For example, Hun flight distance varies with age. Early in September, young birds may only fly short distances and will land in sight of the intruder. As the birds mature, flight distance increases, and usually the covey will put a hill, knoll, or ridge between itself and the intruder and swing out of sight before landing. Older coveys, once out of sight, may follow a course that is familiar to them. The distance of a specific covey flight will vary according to the habitat, terrain, age of the birds, and the weather.

A covey of Huns that is hunted often becomes spooked, and

their flight distance will expand. A covey that has been flushed several times in succession may also increase its flight distance. Much like bobwhite quail, Huns will sit tighter after a covey is broken up. I believe that if a covey has not been hunted often, birds seldom fly more than three hundred yards. Late in the fall, or if the birds have been pursued many times, they will increase that distance beyond a third of a mile.

When working dogs in a field, whether hunting or exercising, I follow the highest practical landforms so that I can watch my wide-ranging pointing dogs work and so I can observe coveys flying to another location. I have witnessed birds twisting and turning left to right, following a landform before landing, and I have observed coveys that fly around the contour of a hill in a horseshoe pattern, landing just one-eighth of a mile from their starting point.

Mobility in winter depends on the birds' habits, food sources, and habitat. I think of covey movements in terms of loose circles changing in radius at different times of the year. In winter, a covey may occupy only a few acres in the corner of a stubble field for several weeks if they are undisturbed, food is available, and all other daily needs are met. At times, the covey's home range amounts to less than three hundred yards. If conditions change due to weather or other circumstances, such as cattle moving into their living space, the circle may expand to the covey's outer limits. Covey circles overlap, especially when feeding areas become scarce.

For years, I've hunted a large grain field that is dryland strip farmed. The field is narrow and about three miles long. Down one side of the field there is an old county road, long abandoned and used only by a farmer moving equipment to and from the field. The old right-of-way is one hundred feet wide, overgrown with heavy grasses and other vegetation. The fence on one side of the lane has fallen down, and sagebrush covers the rotted wooden posts and wire. Across the grain field a long, winding irrigation ditch follows the contour of the land, carrying water to hay meadows below. The ends of the field have deep sagebrush gullies leading down to the ditch. Within the field are several knolls with rocky outcroppings. This large rolling hill country has many deep draws filled with juniper and woody vegetation, some with springs and small creeks. The grassland is well managed and used only in the summer as pasture for cattle. The draws run parallel, leading upward to rocky palisades. This is ideal habitat for Huns. In productive years, four or five coveys use the grainfield year-round. Two live along the road, and the others trade back and forth between the gully and the brushy ditch.

In very good years, there may be twenty coveys of Huns scattered throughout the lush grassland surrounding the grainfield. Early in the hunting season, when the grainfield is freshly cut to stubble, adjacent grasslands are full of insects, greens, and seeds. Only the local coveys hang out around the edges of the grainfield at this time. Later, the road and ditch coveys start visiting the stubble fields every day, as well. I only hunt these coveys once or twice early on when grassland food is such easy pickings, but I return later in the hunting season when other food sources are diminished and the birds drift in to use the stubble field regularly. I have flushed twelve to fourteen different coveys there. When flushed, the grassland coveys may fly as far as a half mile back to their home range in the hills for safety.

My friend Charley Waterman had a similar place. The grainfield he hunted was a high bench with finger-like draws and gullies leading down to several small creeks. Between the draws were hills of short prairie grass, the sides heavy with sagebrush. In September, the coveys were scattered throughout the grassland, but rarely used the grainfield. Later on, birds would concentrate along the edges of stubble not far from the heads of draws.

One day, late in the hunting season, Charley and I and several pointing dogs flushed eleven coveys of birds feeding along the fringes of this large stubble field. All the coveys we encountered flew back to their original homes down the draws and toward the creeks.

Years later, the grainfield was contracted into the Conservation Reserve Program and planted with crested wheatgrass. After the first year, greens grew early under the protective canopy of crested wheatgrass, and the lush vegetation lasted into winter. While the number of birds did not change, the partridge did alter their habits, using the field all year long.

Unlike the grainfield coveys that Charley and I hunted late in the fall, a group of birds I call the Cabin Covey rarely moves beyond its home range of forty acres. I do not shoot this covey, but I do run young dogs on it occasionally. Over the years, these birds have been so dependable that I can accurately predict their feeding stations during the winter months.

The Cabin Covey's habitat consists of two small fenced-in fields, less than ten acres each. Every year the crops are rotated here. The freshwater spring, the brushy, wooded draw, and the lilac/Russian olive windbreak never change. The farmer's combine is old, and grain pickup is poor. The wide fence rows are chock full of tumbleweeds. The 1920s-vintage farm implements, strung around the old buildings, are going to rust, making mowing impossible. Things haven't changed much for the covey since the day the combine was new. Some days, the birds don't stray more than a hundred yards from the old antique horse-drawn double-bottom plow. Food and grit and dusting, roosting, and loafing places are all right there.

The stability of the Cabin Covey fits right into the habits most Hun display. Studies have shown that over 70 percent of gray partridge movement occurs within three-quarters of a mile of a covey's winter range. While seasonal movements do occur during the year, there is no major shift between seasons as with some gallinaceous birds.

Hun seasonal habits and habitat changes are more prevalent in farming regions than in grassland areas. Farmland often rotates from year to year. In early spring on agricultural lands, mating pairs spread out from their winter range to occupy all types of habitat. Later, the adults and young move to growing grainfields and other cultivated lands. In summer, when hay is cut or grainfields harvested, birds spend more time in these open fields. In fall and winter, birds use the stubble and other cut crops more and more for feeding and resting.

The Hun was originally a bird of the steppes, and despite its current association with agricultural development here in North America, I have found that, like its ancestors, it remains a bird of the temperate grassland ecosystems. Coveys may not be as numerous on prairies as around croplands, but they are there. I personally spend more time following coveys in grasslands. Grasslands in the prairies of the U.S. and Canada support good populations of gray partridge as long as the habitat and food sources are stable. Prairies, if managed properly, change little through the seasons.

And the daily activities of the Huns change according to the seasons. If the weather conditions are warm and favorable, dusting takes place along dirt roads and dry cultivated fields early in the morning just after sunrise. In grasslands, Huns dust in open areas and around sandy rock outcroppings. Huns will use the same place to dust from day to day as long as conditions don't change. During the hottest part of the day, the young usually seek shade under brush such as rose bushes, chokecherries, and hawthorns, along hillsides, or even under farm equipment. As the birds mature, feeding is reserved mostly for early morning and late afternoon hours. In late fall and winter, when day length is shorter, feeding activities extend over a longer period in both morning and evening.

Years ago, I would take time out of the bird hunting season to scout or hunt antelope in the "Big Open." Getting in position to view these prairie speedsters meant getting out several hours before sunup. To my amazement, I would hear and see Huns in the predawn light flying to their feeding grounds. Other times, while training dogs or hunting birds, I would be several miles from my hunting rig. Walking back long after dark, I would hear the birds flying from their feeding areas. Sometimes the dogs would point Huns feeding well after dark.

In summer, the birds seek higher ground, and roosting takes place in open stubble and short grasses on the prairie. When Huns are young, the whole covey will roost in a compact circle much like bobwhite quail. Later, when the weather is still warm, Huns roost in looser formations with three or four birds in a circle. When night temperatures drop well below freezing or during snowstorms, Huns form one large, tight circle, their bodies touching and heads facing outward. In winter, the birds may roost in much heavier cover, in low depressions, and on side hills to get out of the wind.

LIFE CYCLE

The Hun is monogamous. Single birds seen during spring are more often a pair (the other bird may run or fly without being viewed). When temperatures warm during late January, Hun coveys show signs of breaking up into loose flocks, with fights among males common at this time of year. Chasing one another and actual combat lasts for short periods of time, but no birds appear to get seriously hurt. In most of their North American range, they begin breaking up into pairs in February. Exchange of members between coveys may occur during covey movements on their winter range. I have observed the tendency for one or more coveys to collect in a recognized meeting place just before mating season. As spring advances and warm temperatures stabilize, the regathering of small groups ceases altogether.

I once worked two coveys of Huns in a stubble field of grass from mid-January to the end of February. Montana can have dramatic temperature changes during this time of year, with highs of sixty degrees and lows below zero. When the weather was warmer, the dogs were finding birds in pairs and in small groups, but when the weather turned cold, they were pointing larger groups banded together in loose coveys. Many times, the Huns would fly in tight formation, but break to land in small groups.

Huns, unlike prairie grouse, do not gather on a lek, but rather pair up in early spring. Since breeding is not locked into a certain area or a peak period, nesting can be spread over a longer time frame.

Weather conditions are indirectly responsible for nesting time. Studies have shown that if warmer temperatures and drier days occur during the pre-nesting season, the peak hatching period can move forward by a week or two. This is particularly evident when observing hatch times in the southern versus the northern regions, which may differ by several weeks.

Other observations indicate that older females nest earlier than younger birds. This is probably due to developmental differences between early and late-hatched birds from the previous year. Some differences in gene pools may also be a factor in the hatching time. While my own observations cover only a small area of the birds' range, they indicate that the hatching period in my area occurs during the first three weeks of June. I have found birds nesting or renesting in late July, but most studies indicate that later clutches have a lower survival rate than June hatches.

The Hun is a prolific bird, breeding in its first summer. Egg numbers in the clutch are greater than that of any other upland game bird. Like all gallinaceous species, it nests on the ground, usually very close to its wintering grounds. Huns prefer to use the edges, corners, and fence-line borders for nesting. However, in grasslands, where years of drought or overgrazing have depleted much of the cover, the nest is more vulnerable to predation and weather. Huns nest along the sides of draws, coulees, and adjacent riparian areas. Of the nests I have observed in shortgrass prairies, all have had a canopy overhead. In one case, I found a nest in a large patch of snowberry bushes. Like nests along the edge of agricultural land, prairie nests have several runways or tunnels through the vegetation. Carryover of vegetation from the year before is an important factor in the selection of a nesting site.

The hen builds a nest from materials collected nearby. The nest's bottom layers are dead grasses from the previous season; the outer layers are dried stems, weeds, and other coarse fibers; and the top layer is soft, fine grass, leaves, and a few feathers.

During the egg-laying process, which can take up to three weeks, the female spends up to an hour each day on the nest. Some days she may not lay any eggs. The average number of eggs is fifteen, but may vary from five to twenty-two. Only the hen sits on the eggs, but the male is close by. If the first nest is destroyed, the female is very persistent, nesting again but laying fewer eggs. Nests found in late July are usually the result of renesting females.

The incubation period is twenty-four days. During incubation, the hen sits almost continuously, although she may leave for a period in the morning and late afternoon to feed, dust, and exercise. As the hatching process nears, she will only leave the nest for short periods.

Males stay in the vicinity of the nest during incubation. Following the hatch of the last chick, both adults closely attend the young, leading them away from the nest. The hen leads, the chicks follow, and the cock brings up the rear. The clucking of the adults keeps the young close by. The female will search out openings so the young birds can learn to catch insects and find other food close on the ground. Brood losses can be substantial during the first few weeks of life. Wet and chilling weather has the greatest effect on the brood, and it also reduces the number of insects, which the birds depend on early in life. Good habitat is the most important factor—more insects mean higher protein, resulting in faster-growing chicks. Good habitat also includes overhead cover that allows the birds to hide from predators.

The hen's most important role is training chicks, while the cock's is guarding against danger. When birds are very young, both parents will use the broken-wing maneuver, flying low to the ground and keeping just out of harm's way, decoying an intruder away. Meanwhile, the young scatter and then freeze. Since they have practically no scent and with the lush, green vegetation giving off different aromas, bird dogs and other ground enemies have great difficulty finding the youngsters. The markings on young Huns, consisting of a light streak down the center of the back bordered by dark lines, enable chicks to blend into any type of cover and hide effectively.

After two weeks, chicks are able to fly short distances. When flushed, they do not follow the adults but scatter in the direction of the heaviest cover. As summer advances, young Huns become more mobile, and their home range increases. Half-grown birds (eight weeks old) are strong fliers and when flushed are capable of flights like adults. Rarely do broods mix together at this time of year, but one or two broodless adults may join the group. As fall approaches, juveniles develop full plumage and are fully grown at about twelve to fourteen weeks.

The brood is the core of the covey, but by late fall, coveys are no longer considered to be true family groups. Small groups that have experienced losses will combine, forming a single larger covey. Unsuccessful pairs and singles also join larger groups. At this time of year, the covey will stay in tight formation when flushed once or twice, but if pursued often, it will break up into the original family groups, which typically land in places familiar to them.

Huns have adapted well to industrialized farming and thrive as long as adequate nesting cover is available. If grasslands are well managed and not overgrazed, the same holds true. The combination of cold spring storms and inadequate cover during and after the hatching period can have a devastating effect on many young birds. If chicks hatch and live through the first couple of weeks, the survival rate is usually good. If a clutch is completely lost, the female will nest again. Studies have shown a female may renest as many as three times if conditions are favorable, but succeeding clutches will have fewer eggs.

Winter weather doesn't seem to play an important role in the Huns' seasonal survival. The birds are able to endure winter storms better than other non-native game birds. Adequate winter food, suitable carryover for nesting cover, and other available habitat is the recipe for supporting good Hun populations.

FOOD SOURCES

Huns have been able to adapt their diet to a great variety of foods, which come from four primary sources: seeds of various weedy herbs, cultivated grains, green leafy material, and insects.

It often has been noted that the Hun is a bird of agricultural regions, where carrying capacity is indeed higher. Furthermore, Huns do adapt more readily to traditional agriculture practices than most other game birds. But they are also birds of open places—the plains grasslands, shrub grasslands, and intermountain grasslands. Over the years, I have made it a practice to examine the crop of every bird taken during my hunting outings. Many of the grasslands I hunt have no agricultural crops whatsoever. My findings are that prairie Huns feed as long as possible on greens and insects. They add a variety of grass, forbs, seeds, and small fruits when greens are not available. If grasslands are managed properly and cover is high, green forbs and grasses are present most of the year, even in the northern regions of Hun distribution. I have found greens and insects, such as grasshoppers that have turned dark brown after freezing, in gray partridge crops as late as mid-December. I have also noticed fresh, bright green droppings while training dogs in January. Green leafy materials are consumed when tender shoots are available in early spring and as long as possible in winter.

Spring foods consist of a large amount of tender leaves, blades of grass, waste grain, weed seeds gleaned from fields and a few insects when available. The young feed mostly on insects during their growth period, later turning to green plants. In farmed regions, the fall and winter diet consists mainly of cereal grains where available, but greens are still consumed. In grasslands with no grainfields present, weed seeds are consumed in place of cereal grains. During winter, if grainfields are fairly close to grasslands, prairie Huns will travel a considerable distance to feed in them, but these fields are temporary feeding places, not established winter range.

High cover throughout the fall and winter in grasslands or cultivated fields makes life much easier for the birds. This is because heavy grasses and other vegetation hold snow off the ground, so Huns can tunnel under it for food. High winds also play a major role in winter survival, keeping ridges and hillsides free of snow for birds to feed and rest. When snow covers the ground, partridge will dive into or dig through soft, deep snow to feed.

Heavy dews, insects, and greens meet the water requirements for Huns. Birds will concentrate along brushy draws and low seepage areas where there is free water, but they gather there because the plants are more succulent around these water sources. Many birds I have encountered in the grasslands are a long way from any free water source and survive on succulent vegetation and insects through the dry season.

NEIGHBORS AND HAZARDS

Since the original stocking programs began, there has been little controversy surrounding the non-native Hun. Landowners have complained about crop damage by ducks, geese, and other gallinaceous birds, but I have never heard farmers or ranchers complain about gray partridge. Huns have never been considered a nuisance. They do not gather in huge flocks, do little damage to haystacks or feed given to livestock, and have no real impact on grainfields.

When the Hun was first introduced and growing in number, there was a reason for concern about the effect of this foreigner on our native species. But there is no evidence that the presence of Huns has diminished any of the habitats of native game birds in North America.

Non-native ring-necked pheasants occupy some of the same range as Huns, but there seems to be little direct conflict between the two imports. The species stick to different types of cover and habitat. The only time they overlap is during nesting season. The possibility does exist that each game bird affects all others in terms of carrying capacity within a particular range, but this is of little overall consequence.

Like all game birds, partridge are subject to periods of fluctuation in numbers due to many causes. While many folks think predation is a major factor, it really is not. It is true that many predators stalk the partridge, as they do all ground-nesting birds. But Huns, like other gallinaceous birds, are such prolific breeders that their enemies do not seriously reduce their numbers. Predation is most common during nesting. It lessens as chicks develop and is infrequent with adult birds. For example, if total losses were as high as 10 percent, nest losses would be around seven percent, the other three percent live birds. The Hun's ability to renest under most circumstances is its best defense against nest predation.

There is a definite relationship between predation and cover type, especially during nesting. Predation from other birds and mammals plays a role in Hun mortality, but it is the type and amount of cover that determines predation levels—sparse cover makes for easy pickings.

After years of observation, it is my opinion that Hun numbers suffer little from predation. Coveys are undoubtedly better at detecting their enemies than individual birds. Roosting in bunches in open cover and a quick takeoff are great advantages in escaping danger.

I do not believe that Huns worry much about foxes or coyotes.

Neither young nor mature birds seem too concerned when pointed by my dogs. In the spring, paired birds hold very tightly, and I have had adult birds hold right under my dog's nose. When flushed, they often fly only ten feet or so.

Once I was walking along a cut alfalfa field next to an irrigation ditch that supplies precious water to a large open area. It is well known that the second cutting of alfalfa is very tender and more desirable as livestock feed than the first cutting. If the second crop matures in time, ranchers harvest this lush green feed in late summer, cutting it as low as possible, but still leaving enough to create short windrows that collect winter snows and stop soil erosion. Gray partridge readily use these open hay meadows if available, gleaning the fields for tender shoots and insects.

The irrigation water had been turned off for the season, and my two Brittanys were covering the field like vacuum cleaners. Making a huge cast, they headed toward the long, brushy dry ditch, pulling up short of the heavy cover and locking up in the hay meadow. I hurried my pace and moved in back of the two pointing dogs, gun ready. I could see the birds moving ahead between the rows of alfalfa stubble. The birds didn't seem concerned with us; they were feeding on bugs and greens as they moved along. The dogs and I relocated, moving closer, but still out of shotgun range. The birds then flushed, flying toward the brushy ditch.

I held up, not shooting, knowing the birds would follow the ditch for about two hundred yards and land on the other side in a sagebrush knoll. Out of the pale gray sky, a prairie falcon, wings folded, came screaming down, putting the partridge on the ground like someone had thrown a net over them. They hit the dirt, running toward a large chokecherry patch along the brushy ditch. Chokecherries have very little understory, but they have a thick canopy overhead. The prairie falcon made three quick passes over the tops of the bushes, kicked in his afterburners, and disappeared into the overcast sky from whence he came.

The dogs were already pointing toward the chokecherry bushes when I got there. I peered into the cover and saw the partridge milling around, refusing to fly from under their protective cover. I moved past the motionless dogs toward the bush. The birds slowly moved a little farther back toward the watercourse and stopped. I backed up, called the Brittanys off, and turned back the way I had come. I saw the falcon working a hillside for other prey; he knew the Huns were safe.

Just as predation from natural enemies is not a major factor in mortality, neither is hunting. In most areas where Huns are hunted, the harvest is less than five percent. With the ability to hatch large broods of birds and an annual turnover rate of 75 percent, hunting under normal conditions simply has no impact on the population.

Predation, accidents, hazards, hunting, and disease are secondary mortality factors. The proportion of population losses sustained from all of these causes is small compared to that of weather conditions and the effect of man's activity on the land. Weather plays a very important role in chick survival. Chicks depend heavily on the abundance of insect food (high protein for body mass) during the first few weeks of life for survival. Thermoregulation (the control of body temperature) in chicks begins to develop in the first six to seven days. Chicks with low protein cannot tolerate low temperatures until they are much older. Wet, cold weather delays the hatching of insects and decreases the amount of food available at this critical time of development.

Farming activities, such as the mowing of hay meadows, breaking new ground in grasslands, burning, and spraying sagebrush, take a toll on birds. Cutting and spraying weeds along country roads destroys nests and young birds. Overgrazing can increase the threat of predators to nesting females. Automobiles, fences, and power lines can also kill birds along roadways.

The gray partridge has a high reproductive capacity, a short life span, and a high mortality rate. Hun clutches, particularly the first clutch of the season, are among the largest of any wild bird species. Natural causes of mortality of all types are factored into the bird's overall survival, but loss of habitat and lack of diversity of cover, with its many edges, are not. Huns, like any other game bird, cannot survive in an environmental wasteland.

READING THE COVER

Huns occupy most of the northern tier of plains grasslands in North America. Their range intersects the tallgrass prairie, mixed prairie, shortgrass prairie, intermountain grasslands, and shrub grasslands. Huns are found in elevations up to seven thousand feet in the intermountain grasslands.

Combinations of cropland and grassland and grassland interspersed with woody vegetation are the most important cover types for the gray partridge. These two combinations may come in various forms, such as wheatfields that have many unplowed edges,

Combinations of cropland and grassland are good cover types for Huns.

Even though Huns are birds of open spaces, they still need this diversity in cover.

rough breaks, and grassy draws. Or it may be a large range of prairie grasslands, brushy draws, and woody riparian habitat. Combinations are essential. If a small portion, one or two sections, of grassland cover is broken up into croplands, birds will readily shift and use the field in winter. It is miles and miles of a single cover type, such as huge wheatfields, that is of little use to the gray partridge.

Woody cover is relatively unimportant for nesting, roosting, and, to some extent, for feeding, but it plays a different role in the grasslands. Plants such as cottonwood, chokecherry, snowberry, rose bush, and sagebrush that grow along riparian areas and slopes and in patches scattered throughout the grassland are essential. These areas are the edges and borders of grasslands. They provide breaks from snow, hot sun, wind, and predation, and they have the effect of both keeping areas open from quiet snowfalls and wind-driven snows. Even though Huns are birds of open spaces, they still need this diversity in cover. These combinations of different covers provide areas for nesting, roosting, resting, dusting, and preening and are sources for all types of food such as grains, weed seeds, greens from grasses, forbs, insects, and moisture.

HUNTING TECHNIQUE

Hunting Huns and other upland game birds (and I don't mean shooting) is much like playing any game of strategy, from football to pick-up-sticks. It takes planning, thinking, creativity, pleasure, patience, persistence, as well as material things. Hun hunting can be casual to complex—just as football can go from sandlot to the big leagues—and like all sports, it should be enjoyed. I'm now in the coaching stage of bird hunting. My knowledge of the birds, their habits and habitat, and pointing dogs is important to me. The end result is not so much a bird in the pot as it is the experience and the memory.

A game plan is essential in any sport. My game plan is basically the same for all upland game birds, but the tactics differ according to each bird's habits and habitat. Break the tactics down to their simplest forms and analyze them. Read the terrain. The number one factor in choosing the area you plan to hunt is adequate cover or habitat. If a grasshopper has to carry his lunch to the field you plan to hunt, forget it. What is the most effective way to use dogs? What is the covey doing this time of day? What time of year is it? (Huns change their habits throughout the season.) How will weather conditions affect the day's hunt? Let me explain.

Much of the topography the gray partridge lives in consists of gently rolling hills, bare knolls, and shallow depressions in an open landscape. Coulees and draws run through open country. Once the land was all grassland, but over the years much of this land has become tillable cropland. Some parts remained untouched by the plow due to the lay of the land—high mountains, foothills, and steep slopes. All lands have drainage to river systems. Drainage in high regions starts as a shallow grassland depression forming into draws, gullies, and coulees that become larger, deeper, and wider as they descend. The draws usually run parallel, forming waterways and feeding coulees that drain into large valleys.

A great deal of the gray partridge hunting I do is in rolling country with draws and coulees running parallel to each other. Whether it be cropland or grassland, a section of land (640 acres, which is one square mile) may have only one or two coulees running through it, but it may have many little draws and gullies leading to the coulees at many different elevations.

A single section is just one part of the arena. Many sections taken together, whether mixed with cereal crops or just open range, comprise the whole playing field. The key is to devise a plan of attack that breaks down such large areas and allows you to use the terrain to your advantage.

Many hunters start by following the bottom of a draw to its end and crossing over to the next parallel draw, never changing elevation except for the rise and fall of the draw itself. This method does work, but they are restricting themselves to only one small part of the playing field. The cover is usually higher along a depression because moisture collects in low places, but partridge frequent the bottoms only at certain times of the day or season. Huns spend a lot of time on grassy slopes in between the draws. For example, if two draws are half a mile apart, the chances of finding a covey in the bottom of either draw for more than several hours each day is slim. If the weather is hot, with the sun blazing down, Huns are apt to be in a shady spot under a juniper with no understory; however, they could also be along a hillside in the shadow of rock outcroppings, or they could be resting in a shady sagebrush area.

Generally, if a covey is found at a certain elevation or at a feeding place at a certain time of day, other coveys will be at similar elevations or locations. Gullies start at ridgelines, draining down and forming draws that cut deeply, creating coulees that run into broad valleys. Most gullies have thick sage or grassy sides and, sometimes, rocky bottoms. Draws contain bushy vegetation and short woody plants. Coulees are wider and deeper, with steep slopes of sagebrush, juniper, and grassy areas with creeks running through them.

When hunting a new location, I first study the lay of the land. Does the terrain fit the criteria of cover and vegetation for the partridges' daily needs? What is the most effective approach to hunting the new parcel? Do I follow a single drainage or cross from drainage to drainage trying to figure out the birds' elevation for the time of day, or do I work only the ridges? What should the birds be doing at this time of day—feeding, resting, loafing, or preening?

Just as I consider the time of day, I also take into account the time of year. In September, young birds may be feeding in open areas on greens and insects. In late November, I work the location I believe to be their winter range.

And you can't forget the weather. Is it dry and hot, or is a cold front coming? Like ducks and geese, Hun behavior patterns change in different types of weather.

What is the most effective way to use dogs? I have wide-ranging pointing dogs; owners of flushing or retrieving dogs would use different tactics. How many dogs should I put down—two, three, four? If the country is big and open, I run four dogs, all with beeper collars. I use the collar more for calling a dog to return to me from a distance rather than for determining its location. When hunting open prairie country, I walk the high ridges or work the tops of rolling hills. That way I can observe the dogs below me at a greater distance, but I also have a better chance of seeing a flying covey land. Being at a high elevation when the pointer locks up is another advantage. It is a lot easier to walk downhill than to march up a steep incline and then try to shoot while gasping for breath. By walking a ridge while the dogs make long casts on both slopes and down to the bottoms, covering all elevations, my chances of finding a covey are much greater. If it is midday and hot, I may only run two dogs in a draw for a short time and return by hunting a side hill. As I walk, I look for bird signs, such as feathers, droppings, and dusting places, and if I find any, I take into account how fresh they are.

Once the covey is located and after the pointing, shooting, and retrieving are finished, I make some mental notes. Did they hold tight? How many birds were flushed—any late sleepers? Were the birds flying low and in tight formations? Many times Huns will continue to use the same maneuver on subsequent flushes.

When a covey is flushed, I concentrate on the trailing bird. Like the kids in my high school P.E. classes jogging around the basketball court, the slow ones always cut the corners. It's the same with Huns. The single, instead of going around the hill and hooking in a different direction just before landing, will take the shortest route over the top of a hill. He knows where his buddies are going to land. The late-rising single will reveal the whole covey's whereabouts.

I also remember the elevation at which I found the first covey. If I have had a successful shot and have the bird in hand, I examine the crop for clues to what the birds are eating. Are they feeding on greens, insects, or seeds? If I find thistle seeds, I look for thistle patches, and so on. I observe the vegetation cover where the first covey was flushed. Were they feeding, loafing, or dusting? Often, the birds will land in the same kind of cover as that from which they were flushed. If I have previously found a roosting area by detecting several clusters of droppings, I take note of that, because when birds are pushed, they will return to a familiar site to reassemble. Roosting areas are like security blankets.

In poor scenting situations, I have witnessed days when my dogs actually stood within a covey of birds and were still unaware of their presence. Sometimes it is so dry and still, and the vegetation so aromatic, that my dogs can't find a sack of dog food alongside my pickup truck (although it's pretty amazing how they can always find my lunch, even with it's in the cooler). But if scenting conditions are good for dogs, finding the covey is easy after the first flush. Seldom do I pursue birds right after they are flushed. They need time to settle in and lay down scent. Often, I will not follow the same course as the birds, but circle around them, using the wind to my dogs' advantage. If I am not successful in finding the covey, I begin with a circle, starting where the first flush was made, and have the dogs cover every part of the playing field. By using this method, my chance of finding a covey increases tenfold. If I am unsuccessful again, I expand the circle, working with a longer radius. As the circle gets larger, the odds of finding a covey decrease.

When pursuing a covey, be aware that Huns will sometimes land, feel uncomfortable, and relocate to a more desirable place. I occasionally have sworn that birds landed in a certain spot and have even had the dogs point there, only to find nothing. They were there, but they left for a more secure place close by. I have pressured a covey three, four, or five jumps, trying to scatter them. Young birds have a tendency to break from a tight formation after two or three flushes. This is probably due to the instinctive scattering they did as chicks when an enemy approached. Older birds stay in a compact unit longer because they are more confident in their home or winter range.

Countless times I have heard hunters say that gray partridge cannot be approached at close range. I am in the field running dogs, hunting, or photographing upwards of two hundred days a year, which provides me optimum observation time, and I can state with certainty that this just isn't true if the cover is decent. In fact, during the last five days of one hunting season I had Huns flying up my shirtsleeves. I worked an average of six to eight different coveys per day during the last month of bird season, with very few coveys flushing beyond improved cylinder range.

Young birds, in particular, rarely flush out of shooting range, nor will they fly far.

Huns will run or fly if the cover is sparse. I have also had a small number of coveys flush wild the first one or two jumps, and then settle down for some close wingshooting. A few years ago, I flushed a covey six times, just out of full-choke range, and I never touched a feather. That year the grass was sparse. Great dog work, though. The birds held well for the dogs, but not for me.

I have also had some terrific wingshooting in windy conditions. High winds cause Huns to fly low and land close to their original location. Partridge, like many creatures, don't like heavy winds, and will seek places that have shelter from stiff breezes, such as hillside slopes and low depressions.

In short, Huns will only fly more than a short distance if conditions warrant it. Those conditions can be natural, like the wind and the ground cover, but they can also be created by man. For example, most wild game birds, and Huns are no exception, get spooky when pursued day after day.

One condition that can help hold birds is the use of pointing dogs, although many experienced dogs that have never hunted gray partridge will get too close and crowd the birds, causing them to fly. After a day or so smart pointing dogs will learn how to handle Huns as they do other upland game birds.

A friend of mine has a very fine German shorthaired pointer and spends most days hunting or exercising his dogs on pheasants. Ringnecks, in my opinion, can be a pointing dog's nightmare, even though many dogs do a good job hunting them. The dogs not only point the birds, but they also learn to trail these road-running athletes. And therein lies the problem. My friend's dog is a master at finding, trailing, and pinning down pheasants, but when hunting Huns, this dog does not make the adjustment to working a moving covey. He points the covey well, but as the covey starts moving away, instead of relocating, the dog works the birds as if hunting pheasants, gets too close, and flushes the birds. This is not the dog's fault; pheasants prefer not to fly even when pushed. Huns, on the other hand, will fly. This is one reason the bird has gotten a reputation for flushing wild.

I hunt pheasants reluctantly with big-running dogs. But I have an advantage over most bird hunters because I have a kennel full of hunting dogs and choose to use my older dogs for ringnecks.

Prairie birds may live in some of the same habitat as pheasants, but they use cover differently for escape. Prairie birds react quite differently when pressured by dogs or man. Huns, sharptails, sage grouse, and prairie chickens all have much shorter legs than pheasants and couldn't compete with them in any race. Upland game birds of the open spaces hold in heavy cover and move in sparse cover. Most times, Huns won't sit tight, like bobwhite quail or planted birds, but will move away from danger. These movements can drive a dog with no experience hunting Huns nuts. Young dogs or veteran pheasant dogs will need several sessions on prairie birds before they are able to adjust their hunting habits to work them successfully.

When observing Huns on the ground during the day, I've noticed that the whole covey rarely settles down at one time. Some are always in motion, looking out for one another. Pointing dogs have to learn to relocate (not trail) several times when Huns are moving. My pointers and Brittanys will start working a covey several hundred yards away if scenting conditions are favorable, and will usually point while still a great distance from the birds. Dogs learn this themselves at a young age; I don't teach them. As I move alongside the dogs, they move ahead, pointing again. This can go on and on for five to ten relocations. I can always tell when the dogs are approaching birds. It's in their eyes and the way some quiver as they work the scent. Eventually the birds will slow up or stop and hold. The dogs know the birds have stopped and go as rigid as a granite rock in a fast-flowing stream.

At the flush, the dogs key in on the birds. While hunting in the field, I do not believe in having my pointers stead to wing and shot. I want them on the flying birds as soon as possible. Why lose time? If a bird is winged, get the dog on it quickly. Huns, like all gallinaceous birds, run, and fast, when wounded. When there is a flush, everyone goes into motion—shooters, dogs, and birds. Why should the dogs be rigid? They should have as much fun as the gunner—like young teenagers, they should be allowed the chase if it's controlled.

My dog, Winston, was a smart Brittany. After the birds flushed, he would follow the covey, not chasing but relocating and pointing the covey again. I used to get angry with him when he disappeared over the horizon, but time after time, I would lean on the whistle—no Winston—only to work in the direction of the flush and see a small white speck a quarter mile away

Most hunters have a strong hunting ethic. The number of birds killed is, but a small part of the whole hunting experience.

motionless against a hillside. If he stayed rigid after a flush, I knew other birds were still present on the ground, and he would be steady until the last bird left. Winston would also stay rigid if birds were visible to him on the ground, and he would sight point the birds the same as scenting them. Many smart, older pointers learn this. He was the father of many of my dogs and both of those traits were passed along.

If hunting a large covey, I take a few birds; in small coveys, no birds. Most states have generous limits, but I think two or three birds are plenty, and not because I worry about bird survival. Biologically, I believe, hunting does not harm the population, but leaving a few seed birds may prevent a void in a particular home range, even though it will eventually be replaced by others if the habitat is worth occupying. Furthermore, after observing countless late-season birds that have been pressured over and over, I believe that it is impossible to eliminate a covey. Winter-range coveys do interact, and when the population within a covey declines, the remaining birds will join another covey. While Huns mix because they need numbers for security, mixing also strengthens the gene pool.

Unfortunately, it seems that if a bag limit is high (my state, Montana, allows eight per day), some hunters have to achieve that goal to enhance their egos. I've heard too many conversations that go something like this:

"How was your hunting today?"

"Great, I got my limit."

"How was yours?"

"Lousy; I only got two."

Such hunters do not realize that limits are but a small part of the whole experience.

Most bird hunters have a strong hunting ethic. For example, I recently had the pleasure of taking two young gentlemen on their first western Hun hunting adventure. They enjoyed every aspect of the environment, examined every bird in hand, and made a point of harvesting only a couple of birds each. These young brothers are seasoned woodcock and ruffed grouse hunters and have great appreciation for all living things, be it flora or fauna and the habitat they flourish in. I'm sure a strong hunting ethic was instilled in them at a young age.

I have studied and pursued gray partridge for over fifty years, and I want to repeat: a Hun covey can be approached extremely close at times. In fact, when shooting, I use a 28-gauge with improved cylinder and modified chokes. Huns can put a great distance between themselves and my 28-gauge, especially on the second shot, so the lighter the gun the quicker the shots. I believe that 28-, 20-, 16-, and 12-gauges are all adequate guns to use on Huns, whether they are fine side-by-sides or hand-me-downs, but they should be light if possible. Fine guns are like fine wines—it's all in one's taste. I happen to appreciate excellent workmanship and have several fine lightweight English doubles. On occasion, I still use my old classic Ithaca Model 37, 16-gauge featherweight pump on Huns. And finally, a dead Hun is a dead Hun no matter what gun brought it down.

For shot size, I keep it simple. My recommendation is No. 7 1/2 throughout the whole hunting season no matter what load is used.

NAMING COVEYS

On western rivers, good fly-fishing holes have names: Burnt Tree Hole, Rockslide Hole, and Joe Brook's Hole, to name a few. Being a fly fisherman, I know that it is much easier to remember a place where I have caught or lost a big fish if it has a name connected to it. This is why long ago I started to name and record the partridge coveys I hunt year after year.

I have hunted some coveys for fifty years. These foundation coveys are there even when the population is down. I name the coveys after large areas, like the Triangle or the Rattlesnake Ridge

Home of the Homestead Covey.

coveys. I then break these foundation coveys into single covey names, using familiar objects or surroundings: the Monument Covey, the Cabin Covey, the Homestead Covey, the Two-Post Covey, and the Plowshare Covey. In excellent years with high bird populations, coveys overlap. These surplus coveys I also name— Homestead Covey One and Two, etc. Each new generation uses approximately the same location and feeding areas year after year; as long as the habitat is unchanged and other factors do not interrupt their life cycle.

THE KEYSTONE COVEY

Toward the west is a long string of mountains. New-fallen snow caps the peaks and fingers of green-black forest reach into the parched grasslands. To the south, the mountains are more pronounced. Higher peaks stand like a fortress against the sky. Rolling shortgrass prairie and sagebrush extend to the north, where the pronghorns live. As grassland diminishes from view, cottonwood-lined creeks twist toward the high golden grain fields and disappear at the horizon.

The countryside was once dotted with small homesteads, their cabins and outbuildings placed along creeks and streams reached by dirt roads and lanes. Life on the range was dependent on good soil, water, and accessibility. Farm equipment consisted of horse-drawn single- and double-bottom plows, making sodbusting a hard task and encouraging farmers to utilize the best ground. Fields were small because it was time-consuming, difficult work to prepare them for planting.

Sodbusters had holdings of 80 to 160 acres doled out according to the Homestead Act. Unfortunately, most could not support a hungry family, and eventually the land passed into the hands of larger landowners. Of the few homesteads that remain, most are isolated and used very little. These secluded, wildlife-friendly tracts are much like they were when the first plow turned over the black earth.

The Keystone Homestead is just that sort of place, named by Jonathan Crabtree, who built a temporary lean-to shack next to a natural spring in a canyon, under a large keystone-shaped rock wedged between two huge boulders in a string of cliffs. He believed that if the keystone let go it would crush him to death. This belief motivated him to work long hours cutting and hauling logs for a cabin and to dig a cistern across the dry creek.

It was the last parcel of land selected. Some said this was because of the unstable steep rocky cliffs, while those less superstitious said it was because of the gumbo road that was impassable when wet. After several years of drought and hard cold winters, Jonathan Crabtree, along with most other homesteaders, starved out, sold the land for a pittance to sheep men, and moved on.

Crabtree's cabin has been vacant ever since. Today, the wedge still holds true above the silent canyon and by early afternoon the rocky outcropping shades the ruined shack's foundation. By evening, streaks of low light pass through the glassless window openings and half-hinged open log cabin door, dancing across the rotten, rat-infested floor. Next to the cabin there's an old metal gate hooked by rusty iron pins anchored to a cedar post. The fence once surrounded a garden plot, but it rotted out years ago, and the plot has grown back to what it once was. When I pass by, I swing open the rusty gate, making it sound like Huns flushing.

The overgrown homestead has many edges of diversified cover, ideal habitat for wildlife to live in harmony with one another. A barn owl family occupies the cabin and a great horned has taken up residence in one of the prairie cottonwood trees along the steep coulee not far from where the old lean-to once stood. Most of the prairie cottonwoods are windblown, leaning toward the east. Others have thinned out and fallen, making hiding places and nests for prairie voles, dusky shrews, and wood ants. Chokecherries, buffalo berries, and snowberries cover both slopes of the dry creek.

Shrub grasslands surround the little homestead of eighty acres. Across the gumbo road a large open meadow follows a willow-lined, snow-fed creek draining to the river in the valley far below.

I found the Homestead Covey forty years ago, and I have known them ever since. The covey mostly hangs around those eighty acres, but their home range does extend beyond into the ranch land.

I don't know when the first pair of Huns set up housekeeping here. I sometimes wonder if they were here about the time the homesteaders moved on. My first encounter with the partridge on this homestead was with a mother hen and her nest. I was walking along that June day exercising a couple of dogs. The dogs pointed, and as I pulled them off, she flushed. A friend held my dogs, and I parted the sagebrush and peered down to count sixteen eggs. We moved away as quickly as possible.

I waited several weeks before I went back to see if there was any evidence of disturbance to the nest. The eggs had long since hatched, and to my amazement the nest was still intact, the membranes cleaned out by ants. One eggshell had been removed and lay outside the nest. Other than that eggshell, the nest was undisturbed.

Early one afternoon in July, I saw the adults and the chicks along the gumbo road, but they scurried in the barrow pit before I had a chance to count them. Later that week, I saw the little covey in the partially cut field chasing grasshoppers around the clumps of sod. The number in the covey had not diminished.

When running dogs later that summer, a cock flushed wild, trying to lead us away. I knew the Huns and stayed my course in the direction we were going. The dogs pointed and the hen flushed, going in the opposite direction from the male. The dogs stayed motionless. I slipped leashes on both and held them to see if I could find the covey brood. Several steps forward, the little covey of chicks flew up, feathered the wind, and lit twenty yards away. Throughout the summer, the young birds occupied the shade around the old buildings, the lush greens along the creek, and the overgrown windbreak.

After first counting that clutch of eggs, I wondered how many of the young birds would survive by fall. The chicks were more than half grown in late August when the dogs pointed in the creek bottom. They flew across the county road toward the old homestead and landed in a tight group. I did not follow the birds with the dogs, but turned the opposite direction and led the dogs away.

As fall arrived, the rangeland on the western side became overgrazed, and the Huns did not frequent it very often. Instead they expanded their range to the east and used the riparian creek bottom and the lush vegetation of the well-managed ranch land more often.

In September, the grass turned golden and grasshoppers were still plentiful. I saw the covey chasing hoppers and eating grit along the road. They did not flush, but scurried down the road. I stopped to watch them. The young birds ran into the grass, and the two adults started calling. Most of the birds followed the hen, but two lagged far behind. The cock turned around and looked at the moving truck, ran back, and called the two young birds to his side. They crossed the road and vanished into tall grass. I drove my rig down the road a little farther and tried to observe them, but they were gone.

Later that same day, I ran two dogs in the cool of the evening to see if I could find the covey. Scenting conditions had improved and both dogs pointed. I walked up and flushed the family. They scattered and landed fifty yards away. I returned to the vehicle with the dogs, put them in their compartments, and started in the direction the birds had gone. Using binoculars, I tried to see them, but there was no movement in the short prairie grass.

I waited, leaning down to pick a freshly grown silver sage sprig, and rubbing it in my hands to smell the fragrant odor. The air was clear and the wind silent. Then I heard a call from one of the adults, and then various other calls filled the pasture.

Huns are not as vocal as many other game birds, but they do have an assembly call to get together. I enjoyed the calling, and it seemed to me that the calls were getting closer. There was an open patch within the sagebrush. This may have been the point at which they wanted to assemble. It took thirty minutes to spot the covey hurrying across the opening to the other side. I couldn't be sure of the numbers, but it was close to the full brood. A little breeze picked up and carried the smell of the sage across the prairie; I could feel fall in the air, and the western horizon was ablaze.

I did not return to the covey until long after the Hungarian partridge season had started. It was late October when I again drove down that gumbo road. Frost had gathered on the tops of the tall sagebrush. It sparkled in the sunlight as the wind moved softly through the tops of the silver-gray leaves. Blackbirds were flocked up, some sitting on the cattails. The meadowlarks had gone and the burrs and other hitchhikers were waiting for the dogs and me. The cattle were gone too, moved to lower pasture, and we were alone with the little covey in the aromatic sea of sage. I never did uncase my gun.

BILL'S PLACE

The two middle letters of the first name on the mailbox are gone, even though it appears to be Bill. The farmhouse and outbuildings look rather decrepit and unused, although the fresh tires tracks around the pickup parked next to the house tell me otherwise. It's high noon and I figure if anyone's around they'll be having lunch.

I knock on the front door and nothing happens. Through the window it looks more like a storage place for old newspapers, catalogs, and magazines than a living room. A dangling single light bulb illuminates the kitchen, but nothing moves. From somewhere beyond I hear a teapot whistling. I knock again, hear the scuffle of feet, and wait.

Finally the doorknob turns slowly, light streaming into the dark hall as the door opens. A small, bent-over man in bib overalls, with a weak smile and a soft voice, says, "Hellooo."

I step back slightly, and answer, "Hello, Bill. My name is Ben Williams, I'm a new teacher at Park County High School and—"

"Come in," he says softly, and I follow him to the kitchen.

Standing in the light, I ask, "Would it be okay to hunt game birds on your place?"

Turning, he leans forward, amused, and says, "Nobody has ever asked to hunt those little wild chickens before. How do you go about doing it?"

"I have two pointing dogs that cover a lot of ground and they find them for me," I explain.

"Help yourself," he says with a big grin, "and someday I'd like to see them dogs of yours work. How about a cup of tea, while I finish my bowl of soup. Then we'll go back by the corrals and I'll point to a few places I've seen those wild chickens."

The county road turns sharply left at Bill's entrance gate. Farther on the road is an unimproved gumbo two-track. It goes down a long incline, crosses a concrete culvert with Willow Creek running through it, then rises slowly to level off and dead-end four miles on at a locked gate. The road less traveled is more for moving cattle and farm implements than for vehicle traffic, although I use it for bird hunting. Much of the year it's impassable from snow or rain. Driving through sticky gumbo is like wading in a mixture of wet concrete, hide glue, and axle grease. You just can't get any traction.

After driving through Bill's open four-strand barbed wire gate, down the hill, and across a sagging wooden bridge, which leaves you with the feeling that at any moment you are about to plunge into the creek, I park next to Bill's faded blue twenty-year-old Ford pickup, with its battered box and missing tailgate, a vehicle used for hauling everything from fresh-picked root vegetables to manure.

The country appears well. Willow Creek runs clear, and Gumbo Flat's faint two-track appears to drift toward the slate-blue western horizon. Nothing much more than a string of barbed wire appears on the amber rolling grassy hills to the east. The northern part of the ranch is high rocky ground, occupied by rattlesnakes, coyotes, deer, and several families of Huns. It is used as pasture during the fall in years when there are ample summer rains. Add the bottom ground and Bill's place is still small, but well balanced, with several small irrigated hay meadows along Willow Creek (hardly enough for feed if there's an early winter) and strips of dryland grain fields.

Bill's pickup tells me he's someplace close by. I have a standing invitation to bird hunt without contacting him, but I try the house first, to say hello and maybe kick a little gravel, although finding him inside at this time of day is doubtful. Next I check the huge Quonset that houses three vintage tractors, an assortment of farm implements, welding gear, tools, and enough old parts to fix every piece of moving equipment within a twenty-mile radius. One of the tractors is gone and large faint tire tracks lead out of the huge open metal sliding doors. Then I hear the deep throat of Bill's 4010, 80 HP, 2-WD diesel tractor. In the distance, I see the John Deere crawling along the edge of the hay meadow that follows Willow Creek. Soot-black smoke bellows from the high exhaust stack.

Walking back to the hunting rig, I'm suddenly looking back over a hundred years of a family eking out a living on the land. A stone foundation marks the original log homestead, the root cellar timbers sagging. The orchard is gone now, the applewood burned in the potbelly stove over the years. The tree stumps stand like sentinels overlooking the larger dilapidated second log dwelling, two feet in back of the newer Montgomery Ward pre-cut house.

Here in this lonesome region a man named John Ingomar carved a ranch out of sheer determination and stubbornness. John married Wynona and raised four kids. Bill was born in a sod-roofed log cabin that his father John chiseled by hand. He grew up with an older brother and two younger sisters. A small-grained boy—wiry, hardworking, and independent, straw-yellow hair never combed—he quit school the last Saturday before his twelfth birthday. This was the day that he and a friend burned the country schoolhouse down while cooking a jackrabbit on an open fire in the attic.

"That was enough book schooling for the boys anyway," said Bill's father, "and they would learn more by working full-time on the ranch. The two young girls could go across the fields to Antelope Butte School on Prairie Road, and it won't be a whole lot farther."

Within a few days the subject of the schoolhouse burning vanished, and nothing ever came of it.

Bill and his brother Tom moved out of the small homestead cabin when the girls got older, sleeping in a World War One–era tent until the larger lodgepole pine cabin got built. It was a cold winter, and by early spring they were more than happy to move into a warm cabin with their own bedroom.

Like his father, Bill acquired a workaholic obsession for livestock, the earth, and fixing things that required steel, welds, nuts, bolts, and grease. Brother Tom's expertise leaned more towards concrete, wood, nails, and constructing new things. All went smoothly until Tom's name topped the draft list, then the two girls had to pitch in, and help do outdoor chores.

Tom served in Europe during the Second World War and came back to work on the ranch full-time. Within days after Tom arrived home, both girls lit out for town life; one married, the other furthered her education and taught in a one-room country schoolhouse, much like the building her older brother burned down. Wynona passed away several years later, and when their old man died the boys inherited the homestead holdings.

With a couple of years of steady wool prices the brothers bought more surrounding undeveloped land for back taxes. They got out of the sheep business when it started to fail, and went into cattle, even though the first few years were even harder.

Neither Bill nor Tom ever married. Bill said that there was too much ranch work for them to find time to find wives. From sunrise to sunset, they plowed fields, planted grain crops, cut meadows, fixed fence, repaired secondhand tractors, worked over old farm implements, and built corrals and outbuildings. They also raised chickens, ducks, geese, a couple of pigs, and a big garden for table use, and never went to town except for canned groceries, work clothes, or implement parts.

In dire need of better living quarters, Tom eventually ordered a pre-cut house, sight unseen, from the Montgomery Ward catalog. It arrived by Great Northern Railroad, and was delivered as freight in two big trucks. Between chores they dug the foundation hole, laid cinderblock, erected the exterior structure, did the plumbing and electrical, hung the kitchen cabinets and some lighting fixtures, and installed the appliances. When the last interior walls got Sheetrocked, they moved in. Over the next few years, finishing the interior was no longer a priority, and progressed slowly.

After Tom died, Bill's enthusiasm for completing the interior faded altogether, and he spent every available daylight hour working outside. In all the years I knew Bill, the hardwood floors were never completed, the jambs, casings, and doors never hung, and the inside walls never taped or painted.

One day, over reheated black coffee and store-bought apple pie, I mentioned to Bill that I liked to hang doors and would be more than happy to help. He half smiled and said, "That sounds like a good winter project." I never did ask him again.

Bill sees me coming, stops the tractor, then raises the two-bottom plow. It glistens in the bright sun. As I drive up, he's already down off the tractor, needlessly pulling clumps of golden prairie grass from around the hitch-bar. I can tell he is waiting to tell me something, or just wants to spend a little time kicking dirt.

"Hi, Ben. About a half hour ago, when I first broke ground, a nice big bunch of those little chickens flushed in front of the tractor. They went that way," he adds with a gesture down the creek.

"Thanks for telling me. How've you been?" I ask.

"Good," he says, "I'll bet those dogs of yours can find them. How many do you have with you this time?"

"Ten, but four are first- and second-year-olds. And they need a lot of bird work."

"Well, that's a good place to start; the chickens didn't go very far. Is bird hunting season open yet?"

"Not yet, Bill. I'm just training dogs before the season starts, still two more weeks to go."

Bill and I talk birds, tractors, and the weather forecast while kicking into the new-turned gumbo. After fifteen minutes or so, Bill walks alongside the tractor, says he better get back to his chores, and climbs slowly up into the yellow tractor seat.

I head out into the fields. After making sure that all the dogs have had their turn working the bottomlands, I follow the lane towards the outline of the old building. An evening freshness fills the air and long shadows dance across the plowed brown gumbo field. Just ahead black rings still spew from the 4010.

Over the years, Bill and I would swap a lot of stories. His were mostly boyhood and ranch yarns; mine were dog incidences and bird hunting adventures on his ground. His place became a treasure for me to hunt, with its overgrown brushy boundaries along the meandering creek, wide weedy fencerows, uncut corners, and unharvested crops. I know it sounds like bad farming, but Bill didn't look at it that way.

One day, while I helped him carry salt-lick blocks from the pickup box to the far corner of the Quonset, Bill stopped momentarily in front of the wide-open sliding door and looked across the half-cut barley field toward the creek and said, for no apparent reason, "I've always loved this place, but the wildlife own the land as much as me."

After Bill died, the homestead passed into different hands and the place lost its unique character and richness. From a high flat grassland bench to the south, I can still look down into Bill's old sections along Willow Creek. They've been leveled clean to the edge of the creek and a huge pivot sprinkler sucks precious water from the spring-fed stream. But in my mind I can still see it as it used to be.

SHARP-TAILED GROUSE
Dancers on the Prairie

My two Brittanys were working a patch of wild rose bushes that bordered an alder and birch cut-over woodland, once part of the original forested Great Lakes area. Extensive grasslands and brushy openings created suitable habitat for sharptails, which prefer open country relatively free from heavy forest cover.

On this side of the brush patch was a large, open meadow of tall grass mixed with numerous forbs. The high-tasseled timothy was still standing upright under a light frost. There was quietness about; only the sound of my footsteps and the distant rattle of dog bells towards the rose patch could be heard. It was early October and my first sharptail hunt. The information I had received from the Department of Natural Resources was sketchy. The spring dancing ground survey showed few birds, and numbers that autumn would not be plentiful. (In the mid-1950s, sharptail populations were declining in many regions of the Great Lakes.) I did not know at this time where my teaching profession would take me, and I wanted to collect a new upland bird species for my hunting list before the sharptail season closed.

Near the far edge of tall grass, the bells fell silent. The dogs were not visible, so I walked in where I had last heard the sound of the low-pitched bells. The Brittanys came into view just as three sharptails flushed. One bird came out low and fast overhead. My eyes followed the bird, my head turning, but not my feet. I twisted my body, stopping the swing of the 12-gauge as the sharptail cleared the alders. I swung back to the other birds that were flying through the tops of the tall birches. My 12-gauge cracked just as they cut behind the branches—good try, but too late. Shaking my head in disgust, I heard the sound of clinking bells and dogs crashing through the underbrush to make the retrieve, but I knew that wouldn't happen.

My next encounter with sharptails came in the West. Of all the prairie birds, the Huns made my list first, then sharptail, sage grouse, and finally prairie chickens—three of them my first hunting season.

Sharptail hunting season usually opens in September across most of the northern plains states, when temperatures reach into the high eighties during the day, cool off in the evenings, and often drop to freezing at night. That first year, bright chokecherries were bending the branches, and red and yellow buffalo berries, clustered together and bursting with energy, covered the landscape along with rose hips, wild currants, and snowberries. Fruit and insects were abundant for chickens of the prairie to feast and fatten up for the long winter. Food was everywhere, which meant the sharptails could be anywhere.

The rancher told us the chickens were in the alfalfa field three mornings ago, but he hadn't seen them since. Ranchers seem to lump all prairie upland game birds together under the name chickens.

My two dogs, a hunting partner, and I hunted the green fields first, then the long, deep coulees and the draws full of berries, but didn't see even a single bird. The temperature was in the high eighties and within an hour we headed back to the truck. After watering the dogs, my friend and I sat on the tailgate eating lunch and talked about another place to hunt. Looking upward I realized that the long sweeping uplift to the ridge was the only place we hadn't hunted. Time was still on our side, so I suggested we give the large, grassy area a try.

We reloaded our guns and started working our way toward the ridge with the hot sun at our backs. The grass thinned as we traversed the slope, and a slight breeze pushed against my face, funneling down from the top. Both dogs worked the wind, slowed with heads held high, then pointed. The dogs moved slightly, relocating, and suddenly there were birds all around us. A blur of wings grasped the wind and we heard the distinctive *lut, lut, lut* sound as the birds gained elevation toward the ridge, skimmed over the top, and dropped off the other side. I missed the first shot—it was the unexpected explosion of rushing air under their wings, and my inexperience with sharptails. I recovered with the second shot, centering the bird in my pattern. A puff of feathers drifted down as the white silhouette fell just below the crest.

My partner already had his sharptail in hand as mine was being retrieved. It was a young male, his feathers soft and white. I studied the elegant bird, turning it over and over in my hands; the partial top knot, dark brown V-shaped marking on the breast feathers, elongated spots on the wing coverts, two distinct center tail feathers, undeveloped air sacks, and feathered leggings on the toes. Finally, I slipped my first sharptail into the game bag of my hunting vest—truly a fine chicken of the High Plains.

ORIGINS

Sharp-tailed grouse remains have been recorded as far back as the late Pleistocene epoch, and the birds probably have been in many parts of North America for thousands of years. Early explorers described seeing thousands where habitat was suitable. During pioneering days, sharp-tailed grouse occupied most of the steppes of the northern U.S. and southern Canada.

In many parts of their territory man has forced great changes, pushing sharptails out of their historic range. In recent decades, many small family farms and ranches have given way to large agribusinesses that intensively farm large blocks of land under one type of crop, overgraze large areas, and remove brush and wetlands. This has caused a decline in usable space for sharptails in some areas.

However, the logging of coniferous forests, along with the opening up of boreal forests for farming, has expanded the sharptail's range in other areas. Land banks, such as the Conservation Reserve Program, which returns cropland to grassland, have also helped re-establish sharptails in areas where they once lived.

To thrive, sharptails need brushland habitat that is well distributed throughout a large area, and environmentally sound farming practices can also provide a productive living space for the birds.

DISTRIBUTION

Sharptails, greater prairie chickens, and sage grouse are listed under the general heading of "prairie grouse" due to their similar habits and overlapping range. Shrub grasslands are to sharp-tailed grouse what open grasslands are to prairie chickens. They depend on nonagricultural areas of brushy cover.

Sharp-tailed grouse once occupied suitable habitat over a huge area in North America. There are several subspecies, each inhabiting

a different kind of habitat. At
one time, these different races
occupied the scrub forest,
grasslands, steppes, savannas,
and agricultural lands of the
Midwest and western plains
of North America. The bird's
current range covers parts of
Alaska, the Yukon, and the
Northwest Territories, along
with six other Canadian
provinces and over twelve
states.

Today, the plains sharp-
tailed grouse is the most
important subspecies when it comes to hunting. It is a resident
of portions of Alberta, Saskatchewan, Montana, Wyoming, the
Dakotas, Nebraska, and Colorado, and historically extended to
Kansas and Oklahoma.

KNOWING THE BIRD

In North America, the sharp-tailed grouse (*Tympanuchus
phasianellus*), has been given many common names: sharptail,
pintail, brush chicken, fire grouse, prairie pheasant, speckle-belly,
white-belly, and the list goes on. There are seven subspecies,
occupying suitable habitat over a huge area in North America.
This book deals mainly with the plains sharp-tailed grouse (*T.
p. jamesi*) and the northern race sharptail (*T. p. campestris*). The
general characteristics of each race of sharp-tailed grouse differ
slightly, but the requirements for hunting them are similar.

A full-grown sharptail is larger than a ruffed grouse and only
slightly lighter in weight than a hen pheasant. The average weight
of the male is two pounds, and the female is slightly less than that.

Sharp-tailed grouse are light in color and have a very distinctive wedge-shaped tail, that gives them their name.

An adult's total length averages sixteen to twenty inches with a wingspan of twenty-six to twenty-nine inches.

Coloring of the two sexes is almost identical: a general color of brown with markings of dark brown, buff, and white. Sharptails differ a great deal from true prairie chickens (pinnated grouse), having V-shaped dark brown markings instead of bars on the upper breast. The wing flight feathers are brown with oval white spots. The back and neck of the bird are dark brown, and the top of the head is blackish-brown—these feathers are erect, as are some of the neck feathers. The central tail feathers are dark with light markings, and the outer tail feathers are shorter and lighter in color. Undertail coverts are white with dark streaks. When the tail is spread, it has a distinctive wedge shape that gives the sharptail its name. Even though the tail is less than six inches long, a great deal of white is visible in flight. Its legs are dusky brown with feathers extending to the base of the toes, forming snowshoes in the winter. During courtship, males show a purple air sac about half the size of a ping-pong ball.

Sharp-tailed grouse are strong fliers, and just as males and females are similar in color, they are similar in flight. The wings are cupped, grabbing the air, and alternating between flapping and soaring. Birds can reach speeds up to forty miles per hour very quickly. When it has reached desired cruising speed and height, the sharptail sets its wings and glides, putting distance between itself and any intruder.

Young sharptails in early fall are usually found in small family groups of three or more. Unlike covey birds, sharptails are in loose groups when feeding, loafing, or roosting, and rarely flush together, instead going in several directions.

Later in the year, as birds mature and become subadults, family groups join together to form larger flocks. Mobility increases, and they travel greater distances in search of food. Larger feeding groups are highly visible, extremely wary, and difficult to approach when feeding in low-cut agricultural fields.

A flock of sharptails rarely rises as a unit, but comes up in singles and doubles, which can present a challenging set of targets for a hunter. Their rise from the ground cannot be compared to a covey flush, or the flush of a ruffed grouse, for that matter. Once airborne they gain plenty of speed. Sharptails of any age that have not been pressured by hunters lie well for pointing dogs. Flight distance after the flush varies greatly, which is true of most upland prairie game birds. Young birds may land in sight of the hunter, usually less than two hundred yards away. As birds mature that distance increases considerably. In addition, after flushing, they rarely land in close proximity to one another, but scatter over a large area. Sharptails seldom fly in a straight line, instead curving to follow a draw, or some obvious landform. Grouse are found in certain kinds of cover at a specific time of day, and when flushed will often land in the same cover type as before. However, if pushed they will seek more protective cover for concealment.

Feeding is easy in late summer for sharptails. Various types of grain, weed seeds on grasslands, fruits, and greens in brushland are all available, leaving little reason for the birds to travel far.

As fall approaches (late hunting season), family broods break up and flocking begins. Flocks are largest in late fall and early winter, with many numbering over two hundred birds.

Winter disrupts their sedentary life even more. Food is more concentrated and harder to find, and many roosting sites are no longer adequate. Because daily travel requirements increase, the flock's feeding and roosting radius expands.

Even though sharptails are not migratory, their summer to winter range makes them seem so. But under normal conditions, their average annual home range is less than four miles. Large flocks do trade back and forth from feeding to roosting sites.

Many folks look across miles and miles of never-ending sagebrush or open prairie grassland reaching to the distant horizon and think only in terms of wastelands and rattlesnakes. But shrub grasslands and shortgrass prairies are complex communities and are, in my eyes, nature's beauties. They're subtle, not sharing their secrets easily.

When hunting sharptails in these expansive open prairies, I think in terms of walking miles. A friend and I once worked a fenced-in section (one square mile) of mostly crested wheatgrass placed in the Conservation Reserve Program (CRP) the first year the program was initiated. The grass was high and the green forbs many. Surrounded by miles of sagebrush, the CRP parcel had been a sharptail, Hun, and sage grouse hangout in previous years. Indeed, it seemed like a meeting place for most of the wildlife in the area. The day was a warm for autumn, and the closest water was a large stock dam three miles away. Packing water for four dogs and ourselves restricted our hunting to only one section of ground at a time before we had to return to the hunting rig to resupply.

After crisscrossing the field several times, we found that the birds just weren't where they were supposed to be. The dogs got birdy three or four times and pointed once, but did not produce any finds. There was evidence that several family groups of sharptail previously used the CRP field for roosting. Why the birds were not using the field as in past years puzzled me. After returning to the pickup for water and a bite to eat, we decided to hunt the perimeter of the crested wheatgrass. Walking through sagebrush can be tough going, but the section lines had grassy unused dirt roads around them, making our travel easy. I believe the dogs liked running the tall sagebrush country, as it shaded them from the sun, and they could stop periodically to lie on the cool soil beneath the big sage plants. We walked almost three-quarters of the way around the edge of the field, seeing only a couple of big male sage grouse flying in the distance. I was sure the dogs put them up. Gunner, one of my Brittanys, came back looking a little sheepish, but scenting conditions also could have been better. Things were not looking too promising for finding birds, when a single sharptail took wing just out of shooting range. Both of us finally realized that the dogs were on point somewhere out of sight in the heavy sage. Luckily, no dog broke point when the single flushed.

We started in the direction of the single, and the dogs soon came into view. All four were motionless, their eyes looking straight toward us, about a hundred yards away in a low grassy swale. We walked in slowly, our 28-gauge side-by-sides in the alert position, the heel of the stocks tucked just under our shooting arms. It seemed as though every sharptail in a two-mile radius had concentrated there, and when we approached, they catapulted into the air in delayed waves of singles, doubles, and triples—like hens being shagged out of a chicken coop window. My friend's 28-gauge sounded twice on the first wave of birds.

He quickly reloaded and killed his third and final sharptail of the day on the next rise. By the time the third explosion of grouse reached the sky, our shooting was over. Birds were still coming up after the dogs retrieved the downed birds, flying toward us overhead and settling in the crested wheatgrass field. It seemed to me that the family groups were getting together early that fall. Maybe they were telling us something about an early winter to come.

Daily activities of the sharptail change during the seasons. In spring, after winter flocks break up, males and females spend their time from predawn until mid-morning on their dancing grounds. Feeding and resting take place midday and last until about two hours before sunset, when the birds return to repeat their morning performance.

In summer months, young grouse feed throughout the day, primarily on insects and greens. As the early fall days grow shorter, food remains plentiful, but feeding habits change, shifting to early morning. Birds rest, loaf, and dust through the middle of the day, and then feed again before roosting. In winter, if normal food sources and cover are not available, many daylight hours are spent feeding and resting in trees. At this time of year, birds can become quite wary due to the lack of protective vegetation they enjoy at other times. But where good heavy cover does remain, I typically have had excellent shooting at close range later in the season.

Remember this: Upland game birds depend, to some extent, on their camouflage as a defensive mechanism. I have walked by rooster pheasants and Huns in a plowed field, and never knew the birds were there until after I had passed. With adequate cover, sharptails deploy the same tactics, using their color to blend into the surroundings and staying put. In the open, however, they will use their sight, flight, and numbers for protection. Sharptails usually spot danger at long distances, and take off before a potential enemy gets close.

A friend of mine from the Southwest was visiting and never had the opportunity to shoot a big, wild rooster pheasant, so I was conned into a late-season pheasant hunt. He managed to get a couple of big longtails. When we stopped to thank the rancher for allowing us to hunt, he told us there were about two hundred sharptails feeding in his cut hay meadow. "Boys," he laughed, "go get them if you can."

I drove the pickup to the far corner of the field, stopped, and turned off the engine, and the whole bunch blew out of there, all going in the same general direction.

My friend Craig said, "That's that," as they flew out of sight over a long windbreak.

"Craig, that's just the place I hoped the flock would go. There's a big, deep coulee about a quarter mile away packed full of buffalo berry bushes about six to eight feet high. I know that's where they landed because there is nothing else around but open fields. They'll be stacked in there like cordwood, and you're going to have a shootout that will equal the O.K. Corral."

I put two dogs down, Shoe and Daisy. The wind was in our faces as we walked to the edge of the coulee. Shoe and Daisy came into view just below us, five feet from the brush, never moving a muscle. We took three steps, and the sharptails burst out from the bottoms of the buffalo berry bushes, exploding like a Fourth of July display at a rodeo. The shooting lasted only three seconds. After the retrieves, Craig walked over with a bird in each hand, smiling from ear to ear, and said, "I believe this is about as good as it can get."

"Craig," I said, "if they've got cover, they'll hold."

LIFE CYCLE

The sharp-tailed grouse is polygamous, and its courtship ritual is interesting and impressive. The places prairie grouse gather for their breeding activity are called leks (a gathering of birds). The display area is called a dancing ground; prairie chicken display areas are called booming grounds, and sage grouse areas are called strutting grounds. All three names are descriptive of how each bird performs: sharptails dance, prairie chickens boom, and sage grouse strut.

As the weather warms in spring, males increase their sexual vigor by spending each morning, weather permitting, on the dancing grounds. Females come later, visiting the lek in late March and April. Breeding peaks around mid-April.

Sharptail leks are usually on a raised location bare of grass; in fact, they can sometimes be on a prairie dog town or in a place where congregating cattle have depleted the cover. Many dancing grounds are reused every year. I know of one dancing ground in a nation park that is on an old trail now turned into a blacktop road; it is still used by the birds today. I know of another that became a calving lot for cattle, so the birds moved about a quarter mile away to a bare knoll overlooking the newborn calves.

The breeding grounds of prairie grouse cannot be described very accurately in words. Being there before dawn to actually see and hear the beautiful courtship activity is well worth the time and effort. If you ever have a chance to see a lek in use, don't pass it up. In my view, it's part of the hunting experience.

In addition, knowing the whereabouts of prairie grouse courting grounds will help a hunter locate birds in the fall. Males and females that use the leks will usually be in close proximity to their grounds during hunting season. In fact, many subadult males will follow the older birds that congregate on a lek in the fall. This fall gathering seems to be a prelude to the spring activity.

Acquiring information about lek locations from ranchers and others who work in the field can be rewarding during hunting season, saving many hours of scouting and walking unproductive country. I know of numerous leks of all three prairie grouse species in several states. While it helps me find birds in fall, it also lets me enjoy studying the birds in all their yearly activities.

The female sharptail begins her nesting activities at the peak of mating season in mid-April. She usually chooses a nesting site within a half mile or less of the dancing ground. The male takes no part in nesting, incubation, or family rearing. The female does it all alone.

The nest is a hollowed-out place in the ground lined with grass, leaves, and a few feathers. It is located among clumps of grass or other protective cover, usually in brushland habitat. The hen lays a clutch of six to eighteen eggs, with an average of twelve. Incubation takes about twenty-two days, and during that time she leaves the nest only to feed.

If the first nest is destroyed, the hen typically renests. Upland game birds are very persistent about bringing off a brood. Because of the many dangers inherent in being a ground nester, renesting is a hereditary trait—a mechanism to compensate for losses due to predation and other hazards.

One fall evening while driving back to the main gravel road after leaving one of my Hun hunting areas, I found the Old Country Road dancing grounds. Two male sharptails moved slowly across the two-track dirt road, sparring with one another as I stopped to watch. Three more birds were on the other side of the trail, heads held high, ready to take off at any moment. Turning the motor off usually settles the birds down and they go back to their dancing, but this time something scared them. All the grouse spooked, taking off toward a muddy little creek across the sage flat and disappearing over a hill.

The following spring, I went back to visit the lek. I parked the pickup, making sure the sun would be at my back on the old, overgrown county road just on the edge of the dancing grounds. It was long before dawn, but I turned the headlights off. The only things visible were a few stars and a ranchyard light miles away. I rolled down the window and listened as I poured my second cup of coffee. Shortly, the cooing started; some of the males had arrived, and at first light the females came in one by one. There were five males and eight females. So as not to disturb them, I stayed until the last two male sharptails left the dancing grounds about two hours after sunrise.

The next morning, I arrived at the lek with the intention of discovering from which direction the females arrived and the direction in which they left. Six hens flew toward Little Muddy Creek; another two I lost in the low sunlight, but they seemed to be drifting to the upper end of Muddy Creek Coulee.

The next couple of days I parked on a high hill overlooking the lek and the coulee, but I had no luck seeing the birds. The last morning I went, I had good light and saw five hens landing in a wide, flat opening along Muddy Creek Coulee. I didn't disturb the birds then, but later that summer, while driving the ranch's dirt road, I saw three young broods in that same vicinity.

The habitat and good farming practices have changed very little in this area, and I can count on finding at least three or four sharptail families every year.

The period from hatch through the first several weeks is a critical time for chicks. While predation does occur during this period, weather is the bigger factor. When weather conditions are exceedingly cold and wet during hatching and early brood days, it causes a serious reduction in chick survival, resulting in a sharp population drop. If this happens in successive years, the result can be severely reduced numbers of birds. There is no doubt that this is the major factor in large bird population declines in different geographical areas. For example, several days of cold rainstorms with a subsequent cold front moving through the southwestern part of a state could be devastating for populations of game birds in that whole area, yet the population could be very good to the north. Also, a late, cold spring without warm days and nights reduces the number of insects available, and insects are an important source of protein for chick growth.

Upon hatching, the female leads the brood away from the nest to open places where it is easier to catch insects and find green vegetation. The brood does not have to travel any great distance, as summer cover is about the same as nesting cover. Indeed, the summer range of the young is rarely more than a quarter mile from the nest site.

The chicks grow very rapidly, being able to fly a short distance when they are ten days old. At one month, the birds are almost fully feathered and are becoming strong fliers. When they reach ten weeks of age they start to become independent of the hen, and resemble small adults in looks and behavior. By mid-September they are subadults, but they still prefer walking to flying. From mid-September to early October, the juveniles will flush readily, but under normal conditions they'll only fly short distances.

One CRP field I hunt regularly is less than two sections of land, about one thousand acres. Before the soil bank program, it was in contour strip farming, planted in winter wheat. It has a large, brushy coulee running through it with many small draws and swales reaching into the once golden wheatfield. Several untouched knolls with rocky outcroppings and sagebrush dot the field. While sharptail hunting was good when the field was farmed, the area did not seem to hold birds year-round. Today, however, the field has a greater diversity of food, cover, and edges. The brushy coulee has stayed about the same, but the grassy field has more cover complexity, and is now used all year long by Huns and sharptails for shelter, roosting, nesting, and feeding. The number of sharptails has increased sixfold since the field has been converted back to grassland. Later in the fall, the birds form small flocks, and expand their winter range a bit beyond the large, grassy field.

I do not hunt this field often, but I work dogs there throughout the year. Surprisingly, not only do the young subadults hold well for the dogs, but so do the adult birds, even late in the year—despite the prevailing consensus that sharptails won't hold as the season progresses. I believe the reason is simple: The field has excellent diversified cover and year-round food sources, and the coulee is full of woody shrubs and trees like snowberries, chokecherries, prairie cottonwoods, and mountain aspen, making a combination that works to both the birds' and the hunter's advantage.

The female and her brood comprise the summer flock. Males congregate on the dancing ground, usually staying until late May. Once the males no longer attend the lek, they segregate themselves from the hens, and remain near their dancing ground until fall, leading a solitary life or gathering in small groups of two or three. Some males return to the lek for short periods of time in the fall, possibly due to fact that day length is similar to spring.

As fall approaches, family units break up, mixing together, and forming small flocks that increase in size as winter arrives. These large flocks are mostly loose social groups, and can disperse into small flocks quickly. Flock size diminishes in late winter, then increases again in spring, unlike prairie chickens, which stay in large flocks from late fall to early spring, breaking up when the weather begins to warm, and the spring courting ritual begins.

I've pursued sharptails for many years throughout the hunting season, and have found many small flocks very cooperative. Later in the fall, when feeding in draws, and coulees full of berries, birds often can be approached within shooting range, and still hold well for pointing dogs.

One year, I was hunting with a couple of friends on the last day of the hunting season. It was cold, with snow on the ground, and the steep rocky breaks were full of buffaloberries. A large flock of sharptails was using the area every morning to feed. My two hunting companions had been hunting white-tailed deer, and had watched the birds coming in to feed on several different mornings, so they called to ask if I was interested in meeting them in a local café for coffee, armed with my 35mm camera. The light was perfect for photography, and the big flock of sharptails was scattered throughout the berries. The opportunity for shooting, with both cameras and guns, was superb.

FOOD SOURCES

Both young and old sharptails relish insects, with grasshoppers being their favorite. While adults enjoy them, young chicks need bugs the first few weeks of life for protein to survive. Even though sharptails eat as many insects as possible, most of their diet consists of vegetable matter. More than 90 percent of their food supply is made up of greens, seeds, cereal grains, fruits, buds, and mast.

In summer, they eat large amounts of greens and insects. Flowers, fresh fruits, and some seeds are also used when available. In fall, when food is the most abundant, the variety of food intake increases. Grains, fall fruits, dry seeds, and fall greens are all consumed. Since desirable food is everywhere, birds can be feeding in many locations. Winter brings a great change in the sharptail's diet and habits. Buds, catkins, twigs, and shrubs make up the bulk of their intake when other food is not readily available on the ground.

Finding sharptails early in the hunting season is fairly easy because the young will be feeding in their summer range cover. As the hunting season progresses, the birds may shift to other feeding locations. The hunter should pay attention to the kinds of food the birds will be using at that particular time. This certainly helps level the playing field.

NEIGHBORS AND HAZARDS

Because sharptails, prairie chickens, and pheasants often occupy some of the same country, it's important to quickly identify each bird when hunting these areas.

The key to identification is in closely observing the different species in flight. First, each bird has a very distinct wing beat. Second, sharptails appear white and plump with a white, wedged tail, and they are very vocal when flushed. The sound is an easily identified *clut-lut-lut-lut*. Prairie chickens, on the other hand, appear dark brown with a broad, square tail in flight, and their sound is a soft chuckle. And the female pheasant appears light brown when flying and has a long, pointed, tapered tail. While the hen pheasant is not very vocal, she will occasionally make a high-pitched whine. Ruffed grouse may live on the fringes of sharptail habitat, but I don't think there should be any confusion with sharptails. Ruffs have a long, fanned tail and erratic flight pattern.

All of these upland game birds tolerate each other well with no serious competition for food or living space.

When flying sharptails appear white, plump, and the wings are cupped for grabbing the air to gain speed.

One interesting study suggests that many sharptail families hatch in a short window of time, say ten days. If extremely wet, cold weather occurs during this period, many young birds are wiped out, causing a sharp decline in population.

Weather is a much greater mortality factor than predation. While sharptails do suffer losses from nest marauders such as skunks, magpies, coyotes, crows, and foxes, it is arguable that predation can ultimately be beneficial, aiding in the survival of the species. This is because nest predation forces the sharptail hen to renest, pushing the next clutch of eggs out of a bad weather window and into warmer weather more conducive to survival.

As with predation, sharptail losses from accidents are common in some areas, although they are not a large mortality factor compared to other game birds that live around farms, ranches, and roads. Some are lost to fences, automobiles, farming equipment, or livestock, but most nesting and rearing of young is done away from civilization. All in all, predation, disease, accidents, and man's hunting of sharp-tailed grouse have very little impact on populations year to year.

A rancher friend of mine was once walking a fence line to find where some of his heifers had gotten out, and happened to flush a sharptail hen off her nest. He called me to see if I wanted to photograph her and the clutch of eggs. He said he nailed a big spike in the top of the wooden post under which she had her nest and marked the fence farther away with his red hanky. He also mentioned that the hen flew back to her nest when he was about a hundred yards away. I waited until after she left the nest with her brood of chicks. All the eggs had hatched, and the shells were still in place. Ants and beetles were cleaning out the remaining membrane. While photographing, I found a coyote trail not far off the fence line with several piles of scat. I examined the droppings, finding rodent skulls, bones, and fur. I'm sure the coyote was not even aware of the sharptail nest nearby.

READING THE COVER

Permanent brushland and prairie grassland are important to sharptails, and it makes little difference what the cover composition is. The key is to have plenty of it throughout their range. The sharptail is truly a bird of plant succession, from open savannah to forest. The bird is very responsive to environmental changes, and much of its habitat is rapidly changing. Man has had a great effect on its habitat, both positive and negative. Logging and forest fires can be beneficial in creating new areas for sharptails. And where brushy woodlands and grasslands have not been severely affected by civilization or overgrazing, sharp-tailed grouse populations have excelled.

The unfortunate thing for the sharptail, in part of its range, is that it is dependant on mixed types of cover. Brushland, unlike wetlands, is easy to develop and is always in direct conflict with

CRP (Conservation Reserve Program) has been a boom to the growing sharptail population.

man's other land uses. Grazing is often intensive, and serious damage is not limited to plains grassland but also affects shrub grassland and other brushy areas that sharptails need.

Following are three important points to remember in reading the playing field. One, sharptails are primarily an open-country or brushland grouse and prefer to feed in open places. Two, sharptails feed on a wide variety of foods, and their diets change throughout the hunting season. Three, daily weather influences feeding times and the kind of food consumed. Sharptail feeding activities change in cold or stormy conditions, and they may not leave roost sites until late morning. On bright, warm days, birds will fly to feeding grounds early in the morning, but by midday return to shady spots and take life easy.

The sharptail's summer and winter ranges are largely compared to many other upland game birds, but like all playing fields, if one studies it, utilizes available information, and travels the different habitat zones of that range, the rewards will be great.

HUNTING TECHNIQUE

Hunting sharptails brings the hunter into country explored by few humans. The country it lives in is as wild as the bird, far from mainstream America. Most people think of the sharptail as a bird of the prairies, as it thrives mainly in a combination of grassland and brushland, but it is also a bird of other regions. Most of my hunting experience is with the plains sharp-tailed grouse, but these methods for hunting apply for any subspecies.

Upland game bird hunting is like any other organized sport. Knowledge of the species, its habits and habitat, is certainly essential to gain an edge over the opponent. A game is won or lost on how well one is prepared for the event, be it preseason or minutes before the game. During preseason scouting, one learns the prey's movements and location. Before the game, one has to take into account the time of day, the turf, and the weather. Game plans have to be changed or adjusted according to conditions.

Sharp-tailed grouse may not be as striking in color or as tasty on the table as pheasants, but they will take you to places where once only moccasins walked. The true pleasure in sharptail hunting, I believe, is not in the killing, but in the beautiful country into which this bird leads you.

I still shoot a few sharptails each season, not just to hold the bird and to admire its beautiful markings, but to partake in a fine dinner of wild game that many of our forefathers enjoyed around the turn of the last century.

Think of the playing field in four different zones: brushy cover, woodland cover, grasslands, and croplands. Analyze each zone with a few basic tactics in mind. What should the bird be doing at this time of day? What is the weather like—hot, cold, rain, snow? What food is the bird likely to be eating at this time? Are the birds in small family groups or in large flocks? What is the most effective way to hunt?

The range of the sharp-tailed grouse overlaps in some areas with prairie chicken, gray partridge, and ring-necked pheasant. The sharptail's home range, however, is much larger than these last two non-native birds and has a tendency to shift around certain types of food as the season progresses. Different kinds of feed are located in different zones. For example, in the grassland zone, sharptails live and feed close to their nesting areas or in their summer ranges early in the hunting season. This habitat can range from open to sparse areas. Water sources may be close at hand and have lush vegetation nearby. At this time of year birds will be feeding on insects, if availably, and lush greens. So when hunting in the early season I look for such places, and concentrate on areas in close proximity to known leks. Generally, if one family group of sharptails is feeding on a certain kind of food, others will be doing the same.

Think of sharptail country in four different zones: brushy cover, woodland cover, grasslands, and croplands.

As the season progresses, cropland becomes available when wheat, barley, and other cereal grainfields are cut. Sharptail families and small flocks utilize the edges of these freshly harvested fields, trading back and forth from grassland habitat to agricultural land.

Coulees, draws, and side hills containing brushy cover, such as wild rose, snowberry, buffalo berry, and chokecherry, are used year-round by sharptails. When food becomes available in cover zones, such as ripe fruits and berries, the birds will concentrate in these places for longer periods of time.

Woodland cover zones, riparian waterways, woodlots, and windbreaks are mainly used later in the season when other food zones become snow-covered or undesirable. Take into account that these zones are not used exclusively at a particular time of the season. There is exchange between all zones. The important thing to remember is that each zone is utilized more often during certain seasons, and also during certain times of day when it becomes a feeding or living area.

I have lived in the steppe country of North America for well over half a century, and I still spend a couple hundred days throughout the year bird hunting, and working dogs on most species of western game birds. It becomes part of you. I have learned many different aspects of the land through the seasons, and appreciate all living and nonliving things associated with their ecosystems, whether it is flora, fauna, vista, or weather.

Upland game birds take on a new dimension when studied year-round, which makes hunting them more meaningful. Many people study upland game birds without hunting them, and many hunt them without studying them. But the person who studies and hunts these birds, and adds another dimension with the use of bird dogs, gains a knowledge shared by only a few.

Look for sharptail signs such as droppings. If found, determine how fresh they are.

Prairie game birds were made for pointing dogs. Sharptails demand the best in good, quality pointing dogs. For years, Southern boys have brought their pointing breeds north to train them on young sharptails in preparation for quail season. Unfortunately, most hunters continue to believe that sharptails do not hold well late in the season. Indeed, it has often been written that the hunter will never get close to sharptails after late September.

Through my experience, I am convinced that this is not always the case. True, a mature flock of sharptails can't be hunted over and over, day after day, and still hold for man or dog. Like most game birds, sharptails become very wary when pushed often. Their reputation for being unapproachable later in the season is largely a function of cover. When cover isn't heavy, they may jump wild, twenty to thirty yards ahead of a flushing or retrieving dog, putting the gunner fifty to sixty yards away before the bird is even seen.

As with any sport, you have to know how to play the game, which brings us back to pointing dogs. First, pointing dogs have to learn the ways of the sharptail. Pointing dogs trained on birds that hold tight, such as bobwhite quail or pen-raised planted birds, will not do well on sharptails right out of the dog crate. Nor will dogs used on wild, running pheasants do well. Late in the season, sharptails will drive these dogs nuts.

This is because sharptails are not covey birds, and a flock is usually spread out while feeding or resting, so dogs generally are pointing one or two birds. Furthermore, while pheasants and covey birds lay down a good scent, sharptail singles do not, as they rarely sit tight late in the season, and will move slowly away from the intruder. Another reason is that if the vegetation is sparse, few upland game birds hold well, and sharptails are no exception. If the vegetation is heavy, the little scent that a bird gives off is overwhelmed by other odors that can confuse dogs. Finally, as stated earlier, late-season sharptails, unlike many game birds, will not let dog or man approach at normal pointing dog range, so dogs have to be cautious, and not push too close. A good pheasant-pointing dog will tail or circle and pin the bird down, but that same dog will bump a slow-moving sharptail. I repeat: sharptails release little scent; vegetation can conceal the birds' scent; birds will flush if pointed too close; and if the same bunch of sharptails is hunted over and over they will not hold.

While every species of game bird has to be approached and hunted differently with or without dogs, it takes a good pointing dog, whatever the breed, to learn how to hunt sharptails after hunting other birds. It may well be one of the hardest birds for a pointer to adjust to because it takes a great deal of time and experience.

Every year I try to hunt prairie game birds in several new locations. I enjoy studying the lay of the land, the new habitat, how best to find the birds, and the most effective way to use my dogs. I plan my trip for the best time of year to hunt birds in that particular area. Once you learn an area, and find the birds, the time frame can be expanded. I would advise any traveling wingshooter planning to hunt a new place, or new species to take into account the ideal time to hunt that location. I hunt sharptails all season, but I also learn the best location to hunt them at certain times of the year. I cannot overemphasize the importance of knowing what sharptails will be doing at a particular time of year. It is critical in finding birds.

Let me explain what I look for in hunting a new area. I've done my homework, and I know what the birds are doing, and where they should be at a given time of year. Does the terrain fit the criteria for sharptail cover and vegetation? Is the brushy cover adequate for each season? Does the sharptail have the four zones in which to live? If it does, I put my dogs down. If not, I find a new area to hunt.

In new country, I'll run four dogs. I seek out the highest ground first, so I can view the whole terrain, looking for the most likely sharptail hangouts. The time of day is important in relationship to the kind of cover the birds are using for feeding, resting, and loafing. Be aware of the weather, and the weather forecast. Look for bird signs such as feather, droppings, and dusting places. If found, determine how fresh they are.

Once you find a sharptail flock, and after all the excitement is over, evaluate what they were doing, and in what type of habitat you found them. If you were successful, take a crop sample. Try to mark the rest of the birds down, or at least the direction the main group traveled. Not only do you have a good chance of finding them again, but the birds may also take you to the next location for that day's hunt or for future hunts. Were the sharptails jumpy? Did they flush in singles and doubles, or in a loose flock? Make sure you carefully observe the last bird in the air, and notice where he goes.

I use the same gun for sharptails as I do for Huns, a 28- or 16-gauge with improved cylinder and modified, but I believe most gauges are adequate. If I had to choose one choke size, it would

If I had to choose one choke size for sharptails it would be improved cylinder.

be improved cylinder for the whole season. Late in the season, a modified or full choke could be useful, but I don't believe it's necessary if you have pointing dogs trained on sharptails. In shot size, my choice is No. 7 1/2 and 6 with one ounce of shot. As I mentioned in hunting Huns, I like to keep the number of loads and sizes to a minimum. Automatic and pump shotguns have an advantage by allowing three shots on a rise of sharptails, but many are heavy, and I prefer using a fast gun with less weight because I enjoy walking long distances. At times I do carry a fine old 16-gauge Ithaca Model 37 featherweight pump that is bored improved cylinder. It is a wonderful shotgun for all kinds of grouse. But as always, gun choice is a personal decision.

NAMING FLOCKS

My gray partridge coveys have names like the Plowshare Covey, but sharp-tailed grouse families and flocks don't lend themselves to such names, so I tend to focus on the places they live, and the time of year that birds frequent a certain area. These names typically indicate large areas: the Sandy Butte Bunch, September Meadows, Box Canyon Flock, the Left Hand Lek Flats, and Thanksgiving Breaks. I've sometimes used a rancher's backcountry road as a name, like the Salt Lick Road.

These names help me document bird locations in my field notes, and compare the sharptail population in an area through the years.

PREDATOR OR PARTNER

It was a picture-perfect point. The three dogs formed an equilateral triangle. I slowly crossed the imaginary line, turned my head, and watched the two Brittanys on each side of me, their mouths and noses quivering, eyes looking straight ahead, bodies standing motionless. Winston was at the top of the triangle, twenty-five yards straight ahead. Thirty yards beyond him, the blue grama and buffalo grass had been clipped by cattle, and above it, five sharp-tailed grouse heads were visible in the alert position. I did not move for some time, watching, and waiting for the birds to take flight.

Out of the sky came a moving shadow, then an object—a male harrier, pale gray with white rump patch glistening in the sun, his flight the meticulous sways moving side to side, his head turning, eyes searching every square inch of ground. The hawk had seen the dogs and me a long way off, and headed over to investigate. Cruising by me, he dropped elevation quickly over Winston. The sharptail heads disappeared in the short grass, and the birds flattened against the turf. The marsh hawk tipped its wings, turned 180 degrees, and dropped suddenly, claws extended, landing on a bare ground squirrel mound. (Most hawks never appear to belong on the ground.)

Man, dogs, and sharptails froze. The only movement was the majestic bird standing like a sentinel. The harrier's exquisite gray-feathered head, with large, fiery yellow eyes and sharp beak, twisted slowly as if on ball bearings, surveying every blade of grass. It seemed as though time stood still.

If undisturbed, hawks appear never to be in a hurry, and this bird of prey was no exception. Finally, the northern harrier lifted from the mound, strong wings flapping, then glided low across the shortgrass prairie. The bright, cobalt sky seemed to mix with the flowing grass as a gentle, fragrant breeze carried the bird out of sight.

The dogs on each side moved first, about ten steps. The gentle wind must have changed the scent path of the sharptails. Winston held firm. I moved next. No heads were visible as I walked to Winston and stopped. My 20-gauge over-under went up, the stock under my armpit, and my eyes focused over the barrels. There was movement behind me; Clyde was creeping up slowly. Our eyes met and he stopped, saliva running down his chin. I shifted slowly to the right. Mac's eyes rolled once toward me, and then back to the drifting scent ahead. I thought about the harrier, the hawk scream sound, and the sharptails in the short cover. They were about to flush. I hesitated, then took several steps. The three dogs lunged forward, flushing the grouse, and the sky was filled with a shower of feathers. It was an easy shot, thanks to my four hunting partners: Winston, Clyde, Mac, and the beautiful male harrier that set the birds down.

A female harrier has a nest close to my home in the country. The birds hunt for mice, voles, and Richardson's ground squirrels. They never bother the songbirds in my woods, fields, or at my bird feeders. At times, she and the male fly close together, working the tall western wheatgrass in search of food.

SAGE GROUSE
Prairie Strutters

Igazed out over the enormous, gray-green-blue sage flats. Like its colors, the sea of sage was deceiving, and not as flat as it appeared. Between the folds of the mixed-brush prairie was a network of grassy swells, riparian draws, stock dams, and alkaline marshes that looked out of place. The color of the big sage seemed to change day by day, hour by hour, and even minute by minute. If the sky was cobalt blue, the sage was a soft, pale blue-green, drawing its color from above. On gray days the sage turned steel blue. Rain brought out the greens. They jumped out at you, as did the aromatic smell, which reminded me of my mother's homemade turkey dressing.

Rain had turned to sleet during the night, crystallizing the landscape enough to cover the vegetation with a chilling, hoary frost. I surveyed the far ridge for movement. It was still dark. Looking through the military surplus 10X40 binoculars, I saw a slight color separation of dark blue sky and black ridge. The mule deer population was down, and had been decreasing steadily for the past few years, but the rolling sage country was still the best bet.

That's what we had been talking about the night before. It was the same conversation that takes place before everyone opening day of deer season: "Where are the deer?"

"Bucks only this year, boys," the rancher said laughing. "There's a big four-by-four hanging out in the sage flags. Seen him most mornings when I'm feedin' the heifers."

"The sagebrush flat to the east?" asked my friend Ben Pease.

"I knew you'd ask," Chub laughed again, putting his steak knife down. "If I tell you, you'll owe me, Ben."

"Like what?" Ben asked.

"Some deer jerky, the kind you make," Chub said.

"Chub, I always give you some," Ben chuckled.

"I know, and I appreciate it. That's the only part of the deer that's any good."

We all laughed.

"Take the lane along the irrigated ditch. Go three miles through the two gates, cross the deep coulee at the junkyard, and park your rig on the other side by the old farm equipment. Deer don't pay attention to that stuff. He should be on the horse pasture ridge around four hundred yards out. Just right for your .270 if it's set for a hundred yards. Hold it two inches over his back; that should do it. I'll hold up on feeding the livestock," said Chub.

We all got up from the table.

"Do you guys have an alarm clock?" asked Chub. "You should be there at least an hour before daybreak."

Opening day is rarely cold in north-central Washington. Cold nights and warm days are the rule in this semiarid cattle country, and 1961 was no exception.

I laid the Remington BDL700 bolt open across the Travelall, and waited for enough light to use the 12-power scope. It didn't have superior light-gathering qualities like the binoculars. The horizon was transformed by sunlight streaming above the black hills. I slowly scanned the backlit skyline, and a silhouette of dark antlers appeared against the golden light. Our eyes seemed to meet for a moment, and then he was gone, just as the bright red fireball peeked over the ridge. It filled the glasses, blinding me momentarily, and casting long, low shadows across the crystalline prairie. The sage became a muted Payne's gray watercolor.

"He's gone, Ben. The big buck—over the hill. Should we go after him?" I asked.

"No," Ben said softly, "he'll come this way down the draw, out of sight, to the sagebrush flats where the does hang out. Be patient; it's only first light."

Ben knew the country; I didn't. He had been raised in eastern Montana, in big open sage country. I was raised in the woodlands of the Great Lakes, and hunting the open prairie was still new to me.

"Concentrate on the flats, sage high," Ben advised.

My glasses followed the tops of the sage, slowly turning 180 degrees. The sunlight warmed the back of my neck. "There's movement about four hundred yards out. It's something sitting on top of the sagebrush," I whispered.

Never putting his binoculars down, Ben turned slowly, scanning the sage flats, then stopped. "Ben," he said, "that's a sage chicken—not many around any more—a big male. Don't see them sitting on the sage often. Must be trying to get warm."

"Is there a hunting season here? It looks the size of a turkey," I said.

"Yeah, one per day. If you shot one that size, it would taste like a greasewood log dipped in sage. Ben, we're after deer this morning, not birds."

After lunch, Ben went after the buck, and I went for the sage hens. It was the first sage grouse I had ever shot, and Ben bagged the big buck down in a deep dry coulee.

ORIGINS

The western U.S. and Canada have been covered with shrub grasslands for thousands of years. Sage grouse were originally found wherever there was abundant sagebrush range. Native Americans were familiar with the sage grouse long before its discovery by the white man. Indian tribes were impressed with this large and abundant bird, naming places and rivers after it, and using its courtship habits in their ceremonial dances. It was also an important food source for Native Americans and for explorers, hunters, trappers, and early settlers in the West.

In 1806, Lewis and Clark's party first sighted and recorded sage grouse in the vicinity of the Missouri River headwaters. As their exploration continued, members of the expedition viewed thousands of birds concentrated around water holes and other prime locations throughout the semiarid plains of the West.

Early settlers waged war against the shrub grasslands through farming and ranching practices. Habitat destruction, particularly in the last fifty years, has devastated the sage grouse population in a large part of the bird's original range.

The decline of the sage grouse was so serious, with extinction a real possibility, that hunting was stopped in many places. Many wildlife agencies became involved in the restoration of the bird's habitat, helping stop the downward trend by improving range conditions, and restricting overgrazing on public land. This made it possible for the bird to come back in good numbers. While its range is small compared to what it once was, it is still an important game bird in several states. The cover in which this bird lives is unique, and to lose this great native bird would be a shame. Sage grouse still need our help, as they face continued loss of habitat due to energy development, agriculture, invading cheat grass, and encroaching civilization, not to mention relatively new threats like West Nile virus. And there is yearly talk of adding them to the endangered species list.

DISTRIBUTION

S age grouse were originally found in country where sagebrush was plentiful; if other vegetation replaced sagebrush, sage grouse disappeared. The bird's existence is tied very closely with the plant after which it is named. Arid shrub-grass prairie and intermountain grasslands exist in the northwestern states and southwestern Canadian provinces, and sage grouse survival depends on such vast, open land all year long.

Unlike most other upland game birds, sage grouse are totally dependent on a single type of plant community. Without sagebrush, this grouse cannot survive. Within this shrub grassland community, their spring, summer, fall, and winter range is quite different. If you remove one of these habitat communities, the bird population decreases, or, in some cases, disappears. For instance, sage grouse wintering areas are usually tall sagebrush in flat country. Unfortunately, this is also the first type of country to be utilized by man, either turned over by plow, or used extensively for wintering cattle. By burning, spraying, cultivating, and severely overgrazing, man has eliminated much of the bird's habitat. Drought years have also influenced reduction of this grouse in some of its territory.

Thousands of acres of shrub grasslands also have been broken up and interspersed with agricultural land. While overall this doesn't appear to be harmful to sage grouse, fewer birds occupy this kind of fragmented space. If an area has significantly diminished nesting cover or winter range, the entire population may vanish.

When a game species declines, hunting pressure and natural predation are usually blamed. Closing or regulating the number of birds harvested in a given year is beneficial if the numbers are drastically declining in specific areas, but it is not the answer to restoring sage grouse populations to what they once were.

Much of the shrub grasslands range is a mixture of state, federal, and private lands. Over the years, ranching has required more and more land, causing federal and state lands to be leased for livestock. While sage grouse can tolerate man and livestock, land and its vegetation must be kept in good condition if sage grouse are to flourish.

Although its range has shrunk, the bird is still found over a large area. Most of the acreage is now confined to just ten states: Wyoming, Montana, and Idaho have the largest numbers, while Colorado, Nevada, Oregon, Washington, California, Utah, and North Dakota have much smaller populations.

Despite the fact that opportunities to hunt this magnificent game bird are limited, it remains a great bird to pursue where populations allow. The size of both sage grouse and the habitat it occupies are matchless, and it is well worth the time and effort to experience this native of the big open. What it lacks in numbers, it makes up for in uniqueness. When hunting, I think of them as a trophy bird—one bird is enough.

KNOWING THE BIRD

The sage grouse's scientific name is *Centrocercus urophasianus*, literally meaning spiny-tailed pheasant. During the first half of the last century, sage grouse were the leading upland game bird in nine western states. Lewis and Clark called this largest of the North American grouse "Cock of the Plains." Early settlers

Sage grouse live most of their lives in a sagebrush wilderness.

referred to it as the sage chicken or sage cock. Later, the American Ornithological Union assigned the name sage hen. Today, it is called the sage grouse. There are two subspecies: the eastern sage grouse (*C. u. urophasianus*) and the western sage grouse (*C. u. phaios*). Both reside in northwestern North America.

Sage grouse attain their maximum weights in early spring before breeding season. A large adult male may measure thirty inches in length, have a wingspan of thirty-six inches, and weigh up to seven pounds. The female sage grouse is a little over half the size of the male, with a maximum weight of four pounds.

In appearance, both sexes are a mottled grayish-brown, with a dark belly and a long, pointed tail. The male is black on the under body with bars of lighter colors. The tail feathers are black and gray with brown spots. The breast is covered with scale-like white feathers that conceal the air sacs. The top of the head, the neck, the belly, and the throat are black. The wings are grayish-brown on top and have white undersides. A white line starts behind the bill, goes through the eye, and ends down under the throat. The sides of the neck have long white filoplumes; legs are feathered to the blackish-green toes; and the bill is large and black.

The female is duller and more mottled than the male. She lacks the black and white markings, and has no filoplume feathers or air sacs. Immature males resemble the female, but are paler in color.

Adult sage grouse are not adapted for running; their gait is only a fast walk due to their short legs and heavy bodies. Compared to pheasants, their getaway over the ground is slow. Despite this, sage grouse will walk, rather than fly, from danger if possible. Many times a flock will fan out, moving slowly, and hooking behind an intruder. When pressed hard, they either fly, or hide. Because their camouflage color is so remarkable, they quickly blend into the sage surroundings. The male makes a short run, taking off with some difficulty, whereas the female takes off more readily. Cupped wings allow the birds to lift into the air. Once airborne, both sexes are efficient fliers, and can reach speeds up to twenty-eight miles per hour.

A good in-flight sex identification is that males fly with their wings horizontal to the ground; females dip their wings from side to side. Both sexes flap their wings to obtain top speed and soar.

Sage grouse feed and rest in loose groups, and rarely flush together, or fly in close formation, although they do usually go in the same general direction. Flocks congregate in close proximity to water sources, which I refer to as greenbelts, in late summer and early fall to feed on succulent plants and insects. Flocks are composed of small, multiple family groups, and are not suited for long-distance flights. As birds mature later in the season, family groups join together, forming larger flocks, and their mobility also increases. Big flocks become more wary, and flush more readily.

Sage grouse are nonmigratory, but long seasonal shifts do occur, the availability of food dictating the distances traveled.

Though not true in all distributions areas, sage grouse quite often use higher elevations in the summer, but as winter approaches birds drift toward lower elevations, using taller sage and windswept areas to feed. Weather conditions also cause movement from one area to another.

Returning from a hunting and photo trip in the Southwest, I drove through miles and miles of prime sage hen country, and never saw any evidence of sage grouse along the highway. Late afternoon, I turned off the paved highway, and followed gravel for several miles to exercise my dogs in a Bureau of Land Management (BLM) area. I gazed out over the enormous, low, alkaline flat. High sage surrounded the perimeter, rolling upward for miles, dissolving into a gray-blue mass, and merging with the green, forested, snowcapped mountains. Although it was February, only a skiff of new snow covered the basin.

Through the haze of the binoculars, I saw dark objects on an alkaline area at the far end of the flat between the sagebrush and a small pond. The BLM sign posted on the wooden fence post read: PLEASE STAY ON DESIGNATED ROADS—CATTLE AT LARGE. I crossed the cattle guard, and followed the snow-filled ruts along the edge of the flat toward the water. As I approached, an artesian well gushing out of the side hill came into view, supplying open water. The dark objects moved away slowly as the pickup came closer. I stopped, and the movement stopped.

There must have been five hundred birds loafing in the sun around the water's edge. Large flocks of grouse grow nervous around any unusual movement, and as I eased the pickup forward their nervousness started again. Their heads were held high, bodies ready for flight. The birds were too far away to photograph, so I watched their antics through binoculars. A pair of coyotes sat high above the artesian well watching them as well, hoping for a meal.

Early in the season, young sage grouse are not wary, and do not present a difficult target for a hunter. In fact, young birds that have not been pressured lie very well for pointing dogs. Upon flushing, they'll fly a short distance, and land in sight of the hunter. Later in the hunting season, sage grouse become a bit jumpy, especially in sparse cover. Like most upland game birds, it's sight-flight, cover-hide. Mature birds increase their flying distance considerably, but they don't fly out of the country, as many hunters believe.

When flushed, sage grouse follow one another in the same general direction, scatter when landing, and rejoin later. They also seek a fairly straight course, going for distance in getting away from the intruder; they seldom curve like other upland game birds. Sage grouse will also put landforms between themselves and an interloper, flying over hills or into a low coulee before landing. When birds flush from a certain density of cover or location, such as a side hill, or bottom of a draw, they will frequently land in the same type of cover or topography. If pushed hard, they have the capacity to fly greater distances than most uplands game birds.

Sagebrush country can seem overwhelming from a distance.

Sage grouse are gregarious birds. Their courtship, nesting, brooding, and winter activities all emphasize their quiet sociability, but their communal numbers vary throughout the seasons.

Essentially, these birds live in a sagebrush wilderness during most of their lives, and rarely come into contact with humans. During summer and early fall, adults and young are quite tame. This is why the early name used to describe this bird in many areas of the West was the "fool hen"—but of course most grouse have been given this moniker at some point. Just like every species of grouse, the sage hen becomes more wary after numerous encounters with man. By late fall, this grouse is a distinctly different bird than it was in summer. Not only is it less foolish, but it flies more readily. In addition, in larger groups they become more cautious because there are more eyes alert for danger. This is one of the reasons grouse congregate in large flocks—for protection and survival of the species.

Daily activities change during spring. Males and females spend predawn to mid-morning on the strutting ground; feeding, which is not a priority, is postponed for other daylight hours. In summer and fall, they are more habitual, feeding at sunrise and in late afternoon. The morning feed lasts about one hour, while the late afternoon feeding time is much longer. Weather affects the amount of time they eat. For example, on overcast or rainy days, sage grouse will extend their feeding period, and in hot weather they delay their feeding until dusk. During the rest of the day, they are frequently inactive—loafing, resting, or dusting. Sage grouse utilize open water and marshy meadows, feeding on succulent plants as they move to these places for their daily water requirements.

After several hard, killing frosts, sage grouse reside full-time in sage habitat. Sagebrush is an evergreen shrub, and provides an ever-present food supply, regardless of weather conditions. In mixed-brush prairie, taller sagebrush is found in draws, gullies, and around water sources, and is used by grouse as a loafing and dusting area. Shorter and more open sage is selected for roosting locations. This cover type provides easy escape routes from natural enemies. During fall and winter, a small flock, or up to several hundred birds may use a single roosting area.

Sagebrush country can seem overwhelming from a distance, as most people think a sage community is all the same. Upon close examination, however, they will discover that it is very complex, having many different physical features, microclimates, vegetation types, and animal life throughout its range. Just because one may see miles of never-ending sage, it does not mean that birds occupy all the space. One single type of habitat will not support a sage grouse population year-round.

Big, open country sometimes demands that you hunt alone, and every year I put in a few days hunting this magnificent bird. One year, early autumn rains had brushed the prairie with the last greens of fall. High-elevation stock dams were thick with ice. Prairie ducks had winged their way south, their molted feathers showing no color as they lay frozen in the icy edges of the lower ponds. Early mornings and evenings were delightfully crisp. The sun's rays cast long shadows across the vast rolling intermountain prairies. Sage chickens had already left their summer range, and were gathering in bunches, so it was not unusual to find fifty birds together, all in full plumage.

Since I had hunted this area many times, I had a fairly good idea where the grouse would be. I drove several miles west of the ranch headquarters, crossed the main highway, and passed the loading corrals in the direction of the high sage flats. This area had been the birds' wintering grounds for as long as I could remember. I stopped and pulled the pickup off the trail, got out, and waited to see if this year's show would be like the last. The heavy sage covered miles of the broad valley, thinning out against the steep hillsides. A dry creek bed meandered through tall bushes. Its filigree of twisted channels and high-banked oxbows created isolated islands of ungrazed habitat, hangouts for loafing, and resting sage grouse within their winter range. Along the creek, not twenty feet from where I parked, I found fresh droppings and dusting holes under the canopy of great sage plants. The side hills continued to be their morning and late afternoon feeding areas, as long as the snow did not cover the lower sage. Midday, the sage grouse would return to the lower flats to dust and loaf. Due to their size, I could see the birds sailing in from their feeding stations, the singles and small bunches coming off the side hill on set wings, and landing on small islands along the creek in heavy sage. On one occasion, a large male sailed over the top of the parked hunting rig. Its tremendous wing beats sounded as loud as a wounded B-17 landing after a bombing raid. Seeing either the pickup or me, the big grouse chose to land on the opposite side of the creek. Not happy with his location, he flushed and relocated on one of the tall sage islands with the rest of the bunch. Sometimes I hunted in early morning along the hillsides, but I never went into their resting sites.

It's amusing to watch these big, beautiful, black and white forms, wings cupped and feathers vibrating, their shadows touching the tall sage before disappearing out of sight—then silence, with only the wind stirring the tops of the seeded sage.

LIFE CYCLE

Sage grouse are polygamous and gather on leks, also called strutting grounds because of the peculiar movements that they perform during courtship. As soon as these traditional sites are clear of snow, which can be as early as February, adult males begin to occupy them. These areas are usually devoid of vegetation and located on raised knolls, prairie dog towns, or alkali flats. I have observed several open grounds located on salt licks, or mineral stations used by cattle during the summer months. In such places, the ground is beaten down over a considerable area, making them ideal strutting grounds for birds. On one occasion, I observed that a traditional lek had become overgrown, so the birds had moved over half a mile to use a barren area around a salt lick used by cattle.

Males come from several square miles to gather on the chosen ground to start their courtship display, which is determined by the weather. The ritual lasts several months, ending in late May or early June. Once their daily activities begin, they prefer clear, quiet mornings, though what time morning begins can be confusing. I arrived at three A.M. one morning and flushed birds off the lek. The males must have spent the night on the strutting grounds. Typically, they become very active between predawn light and sunup, and many leave by eight o'clock, although I have stayed on a lek well after ten o'clock in the morning waiting for the last bird to leave.

Older cocks have their own space within the lek, while subadult males have to hang around the fringes. Most hens visit the ground later in the season, and later in the morning. Breeding begins mid-April, lasting three to four weeks, at which time females leave for their chosen nesting sites.

The male's strutting performance is spectacular, and written accounts describing the complete ritual will never live up to actual observation of this courtship display. When the male starts his strut, his long, pointed tail feathers fan out straight in a half-circle. He raises his filoplume feathers, forming a canopy over his head while he carries his wings low, nearly on the ground. His air sacs are filled, and as he makes several short steps forward, the wings move forward, making a scraping sound. Next, he throws the air sacs up and down three or four times. Finally, the air sac is brought down with a jerk, making a popping sound. This whole ritual is repeated again and again.

While the performance intimidates other males, it also impresses the females, who, when they are ready to breed, select one of the dominant males in the center of the lek. Females often have quite a selection, as the number of males using a breeding ground can vary from ten to several hundred. They congregate in an area of one or two acres.

Because females nest and raise their families in close proximity to the strutting ground, and adult and subadult males often frequent their spring-chosen strutting grounds in the fall, knowing the whereabouts of a lek will help a hunter locate the birds during bird season. One area I hunt for sage grouse has six leks within several miles. Each spring, I make a point of visiting them to count the number of birds and compare it with past years. A few years ago, one lek had over a hundred birds; last year this same lek had less than forty. Numbers vary from year to year because of weather conditions, but overall numbers have steadily declined due to habitat changes. Although sage grouse have had a dim forecast in the past, they are still relatively secure in few states in the American West. Today, state and federal wildlife agencies are working hard to restore suitable habitat.

Female sage grouse arrive on the lek in early morning, and after breeding they return to their chosen nest sites. Most females start nesting before the strutting season is over. Nest sites are selected by the type of sage cover, usually in a dry area where sagebrush covers less than half the ground. Height of the sage used for nesting is ten to twenty inches. Common sage, silver sage, and rabbitbrush are most often utilized for nesting sites.

Nests are made on the ground in a depression, and frequently under a bush with an open space on one side for an entrance and escape route. Nesting areas may be used for many years, as long as the sites meet nesting requirements. If grouse populations are high in an area, nests may be in close proximity to one another.

Sage hens lay fewer eggs than any other grouse species: five to ten, with an average of seven. While the hen may renest if the first nest is destroyed or deserted, studies have shown that sage grouse are not as persistent as some other game birds. The average number of eggs in a second clutch is less than the first.

Most nesting sites are located within a two-mile radius of the lek, typically on summer and early fall range. In the fall, young male sage grouse hang around older males that frequent the lek they used in the spring. Sage grouse country is big, and knowing the locations of leks and nesting sites prior to hunting season can shrink a hunting area considerably.

A couple of years ago I took a new Montana resident on his first sage grouse hunt in an area that has always carried a good population. The spring lek count was up, and that fall there were plenty of birds. It was late in the year, and he was aching for the hunt. I found them on their winter range, and his hunt was successful. He collected one nice big grouse. The limit was three, but I called it quits. One sage chicken is enough for anyone, and our ensuing discussion went in that direction—I thought.

The following year, he found a remnant flock in an isolated sage area. He told me he went back numerous times to hunt them. I thought I had gotten my message through to him the year before, but apparently not. I believe it's important to educate hunters about what is happening to the sage grouse population, and I believe remnant flocks just hanging on should not be hunted. Maybe they can still make a comeback if their home is put back in order. I tactfully suggested again that he not shoot too many birds out of a single small flock, since it was the only bunch in the area. I suggested he should shoot only one at most, and look upon it as a trophy.

I know of several small flocks close to where I live, including the one that he had hunted. Bird numbers on these strutting grounds are few, so I do not hunt these isolated flocks. I do visit the leks in the spring, and train dogs on them occasionally in the late summer.

Incubation takes twenty-three to twenty-five days, and hatching occurs mid-May to mid-June. Like other members of the grouse family, sage grouse chicks are covered with down (natal feathers) when hatched. When the last eggs are hatched, and the chicks are completely dry, the hen leads them away from the nest.

She doesn't take them very far, though. I once found a sage grouse nest with seven eggs, and returned after the chicks had hatched, observing the hen and her brood—all chicks present—with binoculars from my pickup truck. The family was less than a hundred yards from the nest. I got out of my pickup and walked toward the chicks. Female sage grouse are good mothers, and at this time of year have little fear of intruders. The hen came running toward me, trying to lead me away from her brood using the broken wing act. I did not vary my course, and walked straight toward the brood, which was feeding on the edge of a cut hay meadow. When I did not decoy, she flew overhead cackling back to her chicks and warning them of danger. Young sage grouse develop rapidly, and are capable of making short flights as early as one week of age. These young chicks scattered like autumn leaves in the wind as I approached. The hen flew about fifty yards into the open meadow, head held high, watching me, and I never did spot any of the camouflaged chicks.

As with other gallinaceous birds, the first couple of weeks after leaving the nest are the most critical for chicks. If wet, cold weather conditions occur for a long period of time during the early days after hatching, a serious reduction in brood size can result. Loss of insects, the primary source of protein necessary for chick growth, due to wet, cold weather also plays a role in chick survival. If bad weather, and the consequent insect loss occur for several years, a steep reduction in the number of birds is possible. If conditions are favorable the next year, sage grouse, like other upland game birds, bounce back quickly. Very often, hens will nest in clusters, and several broods will be in one area, returning the habitat to its carrying capacity.

As young sage chickens learn to fly longer distances, they become more independent, and mixing, or shifting from one female to another is common. Hens don't seem to mind, or know the difference; I don't believe they can count. The hen (or hens) cares for the chicks for about two months.

By early August, young birds are ten to twelve weeks old, and hens are rarely present. The young juveniles join together, forming larger groups. By this time, young females are fully mature in size, weight, and plumage. Young males achieve the size of a female at the same time, but do not become fully mature until the second breeding season.

The average annual mortality rate for young sage grouse is about 65 percent. The yearly overall mortality rate for sage grouse from weather, predation, hunting, and other factors is much higher, which is true of other upland game birds as well. A sage grouse that lives three, or four years is an old-timer.

After breeding activities cease in the spring, males no longer attend the lek; instead, they gather in small groups, and live rather solitary lives. The hen cares for the chicks alone. Sage grouse broods are not bound as tightly together as most other upland game birds. And as mentioned above, it is not uncommon for young chicks to stray from their natural mother, and join another brood. Some mothers raise more young than their original nesting brood.

The predominant social order throughout most of the sage grouse's life is the flock. The hen's incubation period is about the only time a sage grouse is alone, and even then females tend to nest in clusters. Soon after hatching, family groups start to mix.

During much of the year, sage grouse segregate into flocks according to sex. Unless the flock has been broken up, single birds are seldom found alone. Even when a flock is flushed, they usually fly in the same direction, and land fairly close together.

In winter, sage grouse of both sexes, and all ages assemble in large flocks, and stay together until they start using leks. While these large groups can aid in the protection of individuals, they also make it easier for predators to locate them.

FOOD SOURCES

Sage grouse have the most selective feeding habits, and the most singular environment of any upland game bird in North America. Few people know or appreciate the importance of the sagebrush community in sage grouse survival. Their life depends on it. Without it, there are no sage grouse. Every activity of the bird, year-round, is tied to sagebrush.

Sagebrush is a very nutritious evergreen shrub, and makes up over 75 percent of the sage grouse diet. It is available the entire year, even in heavy snow conditions. The other 25 percent of their diet includes forbs, grasses, and insects. Sage grouse feed heavily on these greens when available, and will concentrate in areas where these plants grow. Some of their favorite greens, when in season, are alfalfa, sweet clover, dandelion, salsify, prickly lettuce, vetch, and rabbitbrush.

Young sage grouse depend heavily upon small insects, such as beetles and ants, which are high in protein, and essential during early life. When grasshoppers become available, juveniles and adults will feed on them. As fall approaches, insect numbers decrease, and young birds turn to succulent greens. If irrigated fields or alfalfa, clover, or hay meadows are within close proximity to sagebrush country, sage grouse will use them.

Moisture is consumed in various ways. If open water is available, sage grouse will make a point of using it. Birds concentrate around springs, irrigation ditches, and reservoirs mainly to feed on succulent greens, but will readily use these free water sources. In sagebrush habitat, dew or rain is not always available, and green plants help fulfill most of the birds' moisture requirements. Snow is used in winter, and large flocks of sage grouse congregate around snow banks and runoff ponds in early spring.

Sage grouse do have a gizzard, but it is not used for grinding as in other gallinaceous birds. It's a thin-walled organ used to digest soft composite family plants, grasses, and insects.

NEIGHBORS AND HAZARDS

Sharptails, pheasants, and chukars occupy some of the same habitat as sage grouse, but in most cases only the hen pheasant could be confused with a young sage grouse. Even though a hen pheasant has a high-pitched squeak, and the grouse a very low guttural sound, neither is very vocal upon takeoff, so sound cannot be depended on for easy identification. The key to identification is closely observing these species in flight, as each has a distinctive wing beat and flight pattern.

One hot afternoon in early September, a friend and I were hunting a large sagebrush bench with a hay meadow occupying most of the level area. Shallow sagebrush fingers led into the cut alfalfa hayfield. Young families of sage grouse would rest in the draws midday, then work their way upward in the cool evening to feed on hoppers in the cut hayfield.

While working three pointing dogs, we walked the upper edges of the draws that extended into the hayfield, and on several occasions we put up sage grouse, sharptails, and Huns. All three species of upland game birds were living in harmony, using the same habitat for feeding.

Under normal conditions, sage grouse losses from predation, hunting, accidents, and disease are not responsible for a declining population. Sage grouse do experience some nest destruction and desertion from predation and other natural causes. Coyotes, badgers, foxes, skunks, magpies, and ravens, to name a few, all play a role in nest predation, but ground squirrels probably are the worst culprits because of their sheer numbers. Natural enemies and weather are the greatest factors in juvenile mortality from incubation through the first three weeks of a chick's life. Death of chicks from exposure and predation mostly occurs when young sage grouse stray from the hen.

Livestock also play a role in the destruction of nest habitat and nesting sites. Ground-nesting game birds renest and have large clutches of eggs to compensate for these high first-year losses of juveniles.

Losses related to accidents around fences, highway traffic, and farming equipment add to mortality rates, but again are not a big factor due to the fact that sage grouse country is usually far from civilization. Loss of habitat, poor range management, and changes in land use are bigger issues. Management directed toward improving or stopping these practices have a positive effect on sage grouse populations.

READING THE COVER

Sagebrush is a woody gray-green evergreen shrub with an aromatic smell of turpentine. It belongs to the daisy family (Compositae), and grows throughout the vast intermountain western states and western Canadian provinces. Sagebrush habitat vegetation is primarily common sage mixed with other sage species, rabbitbrush, greasewood, winter fat, bunchgrass, and many forbs. While sagebrush is not good food for livestock, it provides valuable food and shelter for many species of wildlife.

Much of the intermountain West is referred to as grassland, but the dominant plant is sagebrush, and these lands should be called shrub grasslands or shrub steppes. Shrub grasslands vary in elevation from two thousand to eight thousand feet. They include lowland flats, open rolling prairies, well-watered basins, and broken, high-mountain plateaus. This habitat covers millions of acres and is the most extensive ecosystem in the intermountain region. In earlier times, sagebrush was not as widespread or as abundant as it is today. This is because poor range practices in the early part of the last century occurred over vast areas of the West, and native grasses were lost and replaced by sagebrush.

People who are unfamiliar with the sea of sage often view it as unfriendly. At first glance, it does seem monotonous, hot, dry, and uninviting, but this arid country of the West holds its secrets well. If one takes a closer look and walks into this big open rolling country, senses will come alive to the stillness all around, the smell of sage, encounters with new flora and fauna, and the passing of large cumulus clouds that cast shadows and change the colors of the landscape.

Sage grouse are somewhere out there in this vastness, and the best way to locate them is to know their food sources. This knowledge will eliminate treks through miles of unproductive sagebrush country. Juvenile sage grouse feed on insects and fresh greens as long as possible. Legumes, weeds, and grasses do not grow throughout the sagebrush community except during moist years. When birds are feeding in early morning and late afternoon, go where the green vegetation is—around stock reservoirs, ponds, irrigated fields, and damp, moist bottomlands and coulees.

Reading the playing field for sage grouse is probably the easiest of all the upland game birds because sage grouse are tied to so few plants, although there are still more places in sage country that do not hold birds than do.

HUNTING TECHNIQUE

Sage grouse were once the leading upland game bird in the intermountain West. When sagebrush habitat was at its zenith, a sage grouse flush could darken the sky. Today, there are many places in sage country that are broken up and no longer hold sage grouse. But the places that do can be outstanding.

Sage grouse hunting takes a lot of shoe leather, especially during wet years when birds are scattered throughout sage country. In summers with little moisture, birds concentrate in large flocks around low, moist areas.

Even though the daily and seasonal movements have been discussed previously, I believe it is important to review them, as it can cut the search for birds in a large area by half. When a single species is so closely associated with a single habitat type, these are easy to define.

Using bird dogs when hunting sage grouse certainly shrinks the playing field.

Sage chickens roost in an open space in short sagebrush habitat. They do not use a canopy overhead because it's easier to escape from predators without one. Sage grouse leave roosting areas before sunrise to feed and water, and return again before dark. Feeding and watering areas are associated with streams, springs, reservoirs, ponds, stock tanks, and low marshy areas. Midday, they loaf, rest, and dust in high-growth sagebrush. Daily activities can range in distance from several hundred yards to several miles. During early season hunting, knowing where to find birds during each stage of their daily routine is invaluable.

Sage grouse are flock birds, and like covey birds they rarely feed or loaf unless close to one another. Nevertheless, a large flock of grouse can spread out over several acres, depending on their numbers. Being big birds in large flocks, sage hens lay down a lot of obvious signs. First, look for tracks. Birds tend to take the easy route through sagebrush, and footprints along roads, cattle trails, and around watering holes are highly visible. Second, look for feathers. And third, look for droppings, including "caecal" droppings. These are pools of brownish-black liquid that dry rapidly when deposited on the ground. They vary in size from a small spot to three inches in diameter. The freshness of this intestinal dropping is easy to identify with a little practice, even though large droppings might not deteriorate for months or years. The caecal deposit is very obvious and will help determine if birds are in the area.

I have never hunted sage grouse without a bird dog, although many hunters do so with success. But whether you hunt with retrievers, pointers, or without dogs, many of the same techniques can be applied.

Sage grouse have no fear of dogs whatsoever, nor do they have any fear of coyotes. I once watched a coyote stalking a flock of juveniles in an open alkaline sage flat. The birds fanned out, walking away at a slow pace, keeping an eye on the coyote. Finally, the coyote could not stand it any longer and charged. The grouse simply ran four or five steps, flew thirty yards, and landed heads up, watching the coyote's movement. After another try, Mr. Coyote turned and started to look for rodents. Within minutes, he jumped in the air over a sage bush and came up with a small dark object in his mouth.

Think of sage grouse as a trophy game bird, one is enough.

Sage grouse have a similar effect on dogs. I have seen birds on the ground watching the dogs just as they had watched the coyote. And like the coyote, some of my young, inexperienced dogs do break and flush birds. My older dogs, however, point by scent and sight. Smart pointers learn the ways of sage grouse, and adjust to hunt them.

Early in the hunting season, young sage grouse react much like sharptails, and hold well for dogs. Sage grouse are not dumb, and if pressured too hard by a hunter and his dog, they will become unapproachable. But in most cases, sage grouse see very few people, and so have little fear of them. The exception may be along a well-used country road or BLM trail used by road hunters.

Alkaline soils, and the strong scent of common sage can have an effect on a dog's nose during hot, dry weather, but the same is true in the grasslands or green alfalfa fields. Green, flowering, and dry plants all give off a lot of odor and pollen, and certainly play havoc with a dog's highly sensitive nose. Moisture in the air, or a slight breeze helps immensely. Sage grouse do have a strong odor. In fact, if lots of birds are present, I can smell them myself; it's just like a chicken coop, but with a flavor of sage. Dogs also pick up smells around moist and low grassy areas. Side hills and ridgelines help dogs in scenting birds because sage's aromatic smell disperses faster from the openness and the wind. Thick sagebrush bottoms seem to hold the smell of sage close to the ground just like a fog trapped in a low place.

Later in the fall, sage grouse form larger flocks, and are harder to approach, but this is true with any large group of birds or animals—more eyes, more legs, more wings, more jumpiness. And all upland game birds are wary if hunted over and over. I believe these are two of the biggest factors in any game bird's wariness: frequent pursuit, and the increased awareness of a large flock of birds gathered together. A break in hunting any single covey or flock of game birds settles them down. After a couple of weeks, you can approach them within shooting range again. When you break up a flock of sage grouse, singles will hold tighter.

Young sage grouse don't fly far; maybe farther than quail

because their habitat is quite different, but they don't fly out of the country like some people think. Once I locate a group of sage chickens, I often find them again and again without much trouble. Big-running dogs can be helpful for this. Running more than one pointing dog is also helpful in shrinking open country quickly.

Hunting new places for sage grouse, to me, is like playing a new team on a new field. It takes work to figure out where the birds are, and how best to use your team. If you do your homework and learn the birds' playing field, the open spaces you have to hunt become a lot smaller.

Sage grouse are not migratory, but will travel many miles to get from summer to winter range. In most states that have hunting seasons for sage chicken, birds are still on their summer range during the season. Montana is an exception, having a season that lasts until November. Late season is a real challenge, and much more difficult, as the grouse are not as predictable when on their winter range. Like other game birds, sage grouse can be pursued more than once after being flushed, but later in the season they tend to fly much farther before landing.

I use a 28-gauge, improved cylinder and modified, early in the season. My choice of shot size is No. 7 1/2 or 6 with one ounce of shot. I believe a 16-gauge or a 12-gauge is better for these big birds, but I have always used a light, fast gun because of walking long distances. I know the limited capabilities of a 28-gauge compared to a 16-gauge, but when using the smaller gauge I don't take long, iffy shots, either. I don't enjoy killing a limit of birds; one sage grouse is enough.

THUNDER CHICKENS

Call them what you like, but to Bill they were always "thunder chickens." Bill's place is in rugged, strong, unforgiving country. It lies in the shadow of the Rocky Mountains, where Chinook winds and thunderstorms roll across the landscape unexpectedly, appearing and disappearing like the thunder chickens themselves. Every day thunderstorms form over the mountains, dumping sheets of rain across the landscape of Powder Basin. This year's moisture proves helpful to the young sage grouse, and the population explodes.

The unimproved ranch road to the house and outbuildings divides the hay meadow, and seeing a bunch of sage grouse in the alfalfa when driving to Bill Landers's place was not unusual. He told me that every morning and early evening the birds pour into the alfalfa to feed on the new growth after the second cutting. "It seems every thunder chicken around uses the field to feed," he once said with a laugh.

Before then, it had never occurred to me that the big bird so relished the lush green legumes, one of few agricultural crops they'll use.

Frank, my hunting partner, drives slowly down the lane towards the ranch house. We quickly catch sight of the birds in the alfalfa meadow, surrounded by miles of shrub grasslands. We both turn our full attention to the sage chickens, letting the vehicle follow the ruts in the dirt road on its own.

Landers's hay meadow still lies in the morning shadows of the mountains, and frost covers the tops of the alfalfa. As long as I've known Bill, he's never gotten a third cutting of alfalfa off the place. By opening day of grouse season, the meadow is bone dry, void of any new growth, and it looks like it's been cut with a lawn mower.

Little bunches of family groups are scattered throughout the field. Several big adult males seem nervous about the hunting rig cutting through their feeding area, and wing off toward the Powder Basin sage flats. Still others never stop feeding as the pickup crawls along.

Frank stops the vehicle to avoid hitting three young sage hens standing in the middle of dirt lane. They walk slowly off the shoulder of the road. The birds hardly move when Frank stomps on the accelerator. This time of year, sage grouse have little concern for moving equipment, man, or dogs.

By the time we get to the house, Bill's pickup is gone, and the only greeting we get is from his old, slow-moving cow dog. She barks, following the hunting rig a short distance, and both of my dogs answer cheerfully. We pass the buildings and bounce down the road, which is little more than a cattle path, for two hundred yards until it dips into a draw that leads down to Flathead Creek. Frank turns left toward the creek. The brakes squeal as we descend the steep, rocky incline down to the water's edge.

We sip coffee while getting our hunting gear together. The dogs come out last. The big benchland hay meadow, now out of sight, looms above us. As we start walking, the two dogs are already far ahead, working diagonally up the steep sagebrush grade toward the fence that separates the meadow from the sagebrush canyon. High above, the gnarled juniper fence posts stand like sentinels guarding the horizon.

My idea is to get to the edge of the hay meadow without any birds seeing us. By the time we climb to the top, the two Brittanys are on point. I unload my 20-gauge over-under to crawl through the fence, dropping shells in the process.

The dogs never move, even after several grouse become uneasy. Thirty yards in front of us the land dips into a grassy sagebrush gully, and the birds are now slowly easing toward it. The fence follows the steep incline of the gully to the bottom and up the other side. A hundred feet to my left, the gully stops abruptly at the edge of the hayfield. The gully is maybe only forty yards wide and full of high sagebrush and tumbleweed.

After the last sage grouse disappears into the gully, Frank and I move past the dogs. They relocate and stop, rock solid. I walk past the lead dog, and take two steps almost to the edge of the gully. I hesitate, anticipating taking more steps, when there is a sudden, loud clap of wing beats and wave after wave of sage grouse fill the sky. It's over in a second. Four birds lie dead on the ground while still more continue to rise. The dogs head for the downed birds, but neither Frank nor I reload to shoot again. We already have more than enough.

After collecting the birds, we head back down the sagebrush slope. Not far from the pickup we sit down and dangle our feet over a cutbank above the creek. Lying back on the grassy carpet, we let the sun warm our faces. Landers's hay meadow is no longer in the shadow of the mountains. Our conversation turns to what other birds to hunt for the rest of the day.

"What should it be?" I ask Frank. "Ruffs and blues in the mountains, or Huns and sharptails in the valley?"

We're about to get up and gut out the grouse in the creek when a tremendous roar of wings comes from the direction of the meadow, moving down the steep sagebrush slope. A huge flock of sage grouse thunder over our heads and land on the far side of Fathead Creek.

"Frank," I shout, "I've never seen that many game birds in the air at one time in my life, have you? There must have been well over a hundred!"

With a smile, Frank nods in agreement, and we savor this moment of wonder for a bit. "Let's go find some blues," he says finally, "the dogs haven't had a good workout yet."

Some time ago, Bill got too old to manage the place himself. His children had little interest in the ranch, so the family sold the holdings and he moved to town. Whenever I drive through the small town where Bill lives, I stop to see him for a few minutes. We rattle on about this and that, and when it's time to go he always walks with me to my pickup. Before I get in the hunting rig, we stand around, kick a little gravel, and talk about all the good times we had in Powder Basin.

It wasn't long after Bill left the ranch that the large numbers of sage grouse declined. Miles of wheatfields now surround the old homestead, and the hay meadow is no more. A while back I drove past where the hayfield once lay. A new blacktop highway cuts through Powder Basin now. And today both Bill and the thunder chickens are gone.

Intermountain sagebrush grasslands have been shrinking at an alarming rate in recent years. But a few state wildlife agencies have worked hard to save the remaining sage grouse habitat, not only for the birds' survival, but to sustain good hunting populations. I highly recommend hunting thunder chickens for a day or two. The country, like the bird, is big, wide, and handsome, and to hear the thunder of wings as a huge grouse shakes the ground and feathers the wind is a memorable experience.

GREATER PRAIRIE CHICKEN
Prairie Boomers

My first encounter with this magnificent game bird was in the late seventies on the national grasslands of South Dakota. Our meeting place was their booming grounds.

The Forest Service biologist handed me a map, with the two designated blinds circled with black marker. One was for a greater prairie chicken lek, the other for a sharp-tailed grouse lek. Pointing to the circles, he said, "These are the two blinds you asked for. They're yours until Saturday. Park by the white posts that block the end of the roads. Both trails are about a half a mile from the leks."

"How far is the chicken lek from town?" I asked.

"That lek is about twenty-five miles. The grouse lek is about twenty-two miles. You should be at the blind by four A.M. The drive takes about an hour," he advised.

"I'm going to drive the blinds today, and check out the roads and landmarks," I said.

"That's a good idea," he answered. "It'll save you valuable time. Sure hope the weather is clear for you tomorrow morning."

Things always look different in the dark. I drove down the dirt road, which seemed to take forever. Finally, the white post came into view. I pulled over and turned off the lights. Total darkness. The only thing visible was a lone ranchyard light miles away. After several minutes, the Milky Way's multitude of stars seemed to cast a soft glow on the landscape. It was three-thirty. Armed with a thermos of coffee, camera gear, chair, and a small flashlight, I started down the faint trail toward the lek, which was on an old prairie dog town. It wasn't long before the outline of the blind came into view. As I approached, several chickens flushed from the booming grounds.

It was even darker inside the wooden blind, and all was quiet except for a light breeze that moved the black canvas curtains covering the lookout ports. Half an hour passed before a lowing humming sound broke the silence. The incoming birds were probably the males I had flushed, now returning to the lek. It was still an hour before first light, and another before I could photograph. My thermos was almost empty when the booming started. At dawn, a single female flew in; the low cooing volume increased.

The sound is enchanting, but the booming ground display is spectacular.

The male prairie chicken starts his performance by running a short distance, stops abruptly, and rapidly stamps his feet, turning in a semicircle. His bright orange air sacs then inflate, and the orange eyebrows are emphasized. His long neck feathers tower above his head. At the same instant, he suddenly fans and clicks his tail. Then the low booming begins.

Each cock defends a small territory on the lek. Two males will often confront each other, head to head, and stop at an imaginary line. Harmless sparing, wing scraping, cackles, and short skirmishes then break out. A few feathers fly, but little harm is done. They stop, stare at one another, and settle down a few feet apart to talk it over.

Most of the birds are typically gone by eight o'clock, but that morning eight males stayed much later, just laying around and sunning themselves. By ten o'clock it was hot, and the last male finally left when a red fox came by to check out the prairie dog population.

The spring prairie chicken count was encouraging. I had figured on going to the Sandhill country of Nebraska the coming fall, but the number of birds on the grasslands leks was impressive. As it turned out, in late summer I inquired about the Flint Hills of Kansas, the Sandhills of Nebraska, and the Missouri River Breaks of South Dakota. All three reports were good.

South Dakota's outdoor media relations specialist in Pierre assured me that there were plenty of chickens.

"Don't come opening weekend of the season, too many hunters," he said. "A week later, and you'll have the place to yourself."

I set a date for late September—and I wasn't disappointed.

ORIGINS

The pinnated grouse once inhabited most of the midcontinental prairie grasslands of North America. Pinnated grouse are usually associated with tallgrass and mixed prairie, whereas sharp-tailed grouse are found in greater numbers in shortgrass and mixed prairie.

There are two species of pinnated grouse, the great and lesser pinnated. The lesser prairie chicken's range is small compared to the greater, and it lives in a much drier climate. This book deals only with the greater prairie chicken, henceforth referred to as prairie chicken, or just chicken.

The prairie chicken's original range extended across much of the central plains states. When settlers first moved west and turned over the prairie's black earth for grain crops, the prairie chicken followed. Between the late 1800s and early 1900s, the prairie chicken population increased at an incredible rate, but when agricultural crops surpassed the grasslands in acreage, the bird's population plummeted. While the market hunter contributed to the prairie chicken's demise as well, it was the plow, not the gun, which had the most profound effect on population.

DISTRIBUTION

Outside of the pigeon family, the prairie chicken seems to have been the upland game bird most affected by man's use of the land. Prairie chickens initially thrived when grasslands were plowed and planted with small grains, moving into places where sharp-tailed grouse lived. In fact, for several decades, prairie

chickens flourished in the interior grasslands, replacing sharptails altogether in some areas.

Eventually, this perfect balance tilted. Most of the native grasslands were tilled under and converted to cereal crops, and it was this change in habitat that caused the decline in prairie chicken populations. All prairie grouse need grasslands. They provide the three most important elements for survival: dense nesting cover, sparse booming grounds, and thick roosting cover. This is why small parcels of agricultural land interwoven through grasslands are helpful to chickens, while miles and miles of tilled land are useless.

Nebraska, Kansas, and South Dakota continue to have good populations, with long hunting seasons for a mixed bag of prairie grouse. Today, the prairie chicken's range is but a small fraction of what it once was.

KNOWING THE BIRD

The greater prairie chicken's scientific name is *Tympanuchus cupido pinnatus*. Pinnates are the elongated, blackish neck feathers arranged on each side of the bird's throat. While both sexes have them, the male's pinnates are longer and are displayed upright and over the head during courtship.

Early settlers referred to prairie chickens as "wild chickens" or "yellow legs." Names used today are prairie grouse, prairie chicken, squaretail, or simply chicken. The recurring name "chicken" fits the bird well, because of all the prairie game birds, it's the most chicken-like.

Prairie chickens are slightly larger than their cousin, the sharp-tailed grouse. The adult male can weigh up to two and a half pounds, reach twenty inches in length, and have a wingspan of twenty-eight inches. The female is lighter in weight and smaller in size.

Plumage is similar in appearance in both sexes, with the upper parts darkly barred and the underparts lightly barred. However, the male has broken crossbarring of alternating light and dark browns over most of his body and a continuous dark band at the end of the tail, while the female has much paler barring and an unbanded tail.

The male prairie chicken also has a yellow comb above the eyes and exposed yellow skin below his pinnates. During courtship, his air sacs and comb become enlarged, turning bright yellow-orange.

Being in open grasslands, chickens can reach speeds of up to forty miles per hour in flight.

Both sexes have tails that are somewhat square, and legs feathered to the feet, which are yellow and slightly webbed on the toes.

The prairie chicken does not migrate. Years ago, when the bird's range was widespread, breeding and wintering grounds were sometimes one hundred miles apart. But unlike true migratory birds, not all prairie grouse in an area would leave. Now, because their range is diminished, prairie chickens do not travel great distances as they once did. While the birds still have seasonal shifts due to weather, available food, and the amount of nesting habitat, they are much more confined than their ancestors were, often having a range that covers less than five miles.

More adapted to flying than walking, prairie chickens generally fly between their daily activity sites. If a ground predator pursues them, the bird will also fly rather than run. But since overhead predators present a different problem, flying is not always an option. Like other prairie grouse, they rely on sight, sound, and camouflage before flight.

Prairie chickens can reach speeds of up to forty miles per hour in flight. The wing is short, strong, designed for speed, and can sustain long-distance flying. The bird flies low and fairly straight to its destination, with wing motions alternating between flapping and soaring.

Even though the prairie chicken is gregarious, flock size depends on the time of year. This is because during nesting and breeding the birds travel singly, but when feeding and roosting they travel in small to large flocks.

Prairie chickens have many vocal sounds to communicate with one another. Most sounds made by the male are used during the breeding season. The more talkative brood female and her young have many calls, and make vocal contact throughout the day.

For prairie chickens, spring may start as early as January. If the weather turns warm, large flocks start to break up, and males begin to visit their booming grounds. If the weather turns cold again, visits to breeding grounds are suspended, and flocks rejoin. This mixing can last several months, depending on the weather. By March, the mixing movement is over, and large flocks disperse into smaller groups of the same sex.

The seasonal mating period reaches its peak in early April, and lasts about two weeks. When booming season draws to a close, males spend time alone, or in very small groups, while females have the responsibility of rearing the young alone. A mother and her brood, with some mixing of other broods, stay together until fall.

At ten to twelve weeks of age, young prairie chickens begin forming small flocks, as single broods join together. These small groups tend to separate according to sex, but with chickens this does not seem as prevalent as with other grouse. Young males join adult cocks, and utilize the booming grounds. Not all males participate in the fall activity, which is more of a relaxed gathering than an enthusiastic endeavor.

Adult and juvenile hens of the year gather in large flocks and remain near the booming grounds, inhabiting a larger area than males. The females' daily movements during this time vary according to type of range. Some restrict themselves to less than a square mile; others start to range over a much larger area, depending upon where the booming grounds are in relation to feeding and roosting places.

If winter weather becomes severe, the sexes unite and form large flocks. The daily cruising range for food and good roosting cover may be several miles. In a mild winter, the flock size may be smaller, and distances to good food sources and roosting cover may be much reduced.

Early in the hunting season, young chickens are not wary, and lie well for dogs. Upon flushing, young birds often fly only a short distance, and may land in sight of the hunter. Of course, my perception of a short distance on the open prairie is not the same as when hunting a forested area. All upland game birds of open spaces fly farther than birds that live in a canopy of cover. In most cases, prairie game birds do one of several things when flushed. While feeding, they may seek cover familiar to them, such as resting and lofting areas, or if hard pressed, roosting sites. If not feeding, they will seek the same type of cover in which to land (for example, shortgrass to shortgrass). If pushed, they will seek heavier cover with some type of canopy overhead. Unlike pheasants, which are runners, prairie game birds usually alight, and stay fairly close to their landing site, although when pursued they may move quite some distance.

Most upland game birds may be pursued after the first flush, and many birds may be pursued after several flushes. Chickens are no exception. I once flushed and pursued a large flock of chickens five times. This bunch of birds did not break up, and even returned once to their original position. While I did finally get a good shot off, it took the dogs and me over an hour.

Most of the year, prairie chickens will not fly out of the country, but will stay locked into a reasonable space. When chickens flush, they usually scatter, but generally go in the same direction. Sleepers, birds that get up after the main bunch, are common, and often follow the main group.

Of all the prairie grouse, prairie chickens bunch up the earliest, and tend to form the largest flocks. Later in the hunting season, large groups are very difficult to hunt. An exception is in late fall, when a big flock travels a direct route from roosting to feeding areas. If a hunter can locate this flyway, he can pass-shoot birds.

LIFE CYCLE

As soon as the leks, or booming grounds, are clear of winter snow, male prairie chickens will frequent the area. During the height of breeding season, males arrive well before first light, with a low vocal cooing sound (*c-a o o o-woo woo*) announcing their arrival. On a clear morning, this sound can be heard for over a mile.

The booming grounds are usually located on a raised area that is bare of grass. Many of these sites have been used for generations, and bird numbers on each vary considerably, with some grounds having as few as six males, and others well over a hundred.

The male's display seems to serve two purposes: to announce his vitality, and to secure his territory on the lek. Males from several miles around assemble on the leks, with weather determining how active they become each morning. Dominant cocks occupy choice spaces within the lek, and subadult males hang around the periphery. This ritual lasts several months, and ends in early June.

Females arrive on the breeding ground much later in spring than males, and much later in the morning. For the majority of hens, the breeding window is only about two weeks. After breeding, they leave for their nesting sites.

Several years ago, I visited two chicken leks in the grasslands of South Dakota. On the first morning, the larger of the two leks had twenty male prairie chickens, nine female chickens, three male sharptails, two hen sharptails, and one hybrid male. The hybrid's territory was on the fringe of the lek close to the wooden blind, and getting photos of him was relatively easy. He was fully barred, and displayed like a prairie chicken, but the pinnate neck feathers were short, the air sacs were purple, and the tail was pointed like a sharptail. The hybrid, I assumed, was a first-year bird. He had a few skirmishes and confrontations with a male prairie chicken for space, but no contact with any hens.

Females start nesting long before males leave the booming grounds. Distance from the nest site to a breeding hen's lek is usually less than a mile, and may bypass other leks that are closer.

Nest location is the most important decision a female grouse makes. First-year females are possibly less successful than experienced adults in finding safe nesting sites. Nest sites are selected by the amount of carryover cover available, and by how far they are from potential predator hot spots. Ground-nesting areas are used for years if the habitat is not destroyed, and it still fits the bird's requirements for safe nesting.

Nesting for the greater prairie chicken begins in early May. While areas used for nesting sites may be partly open, there must be dense clumps of cover and brush. The hen seeks out a nesting site in prairie grasslands with thick vertical cover for concealment. Prairie chickens do not nest in clusters, but two or more hens may nest in the same vicinity.

The hen forms a shallow bowl, and lines the nest with dead grass, leaves, and feathers. As a rule, she lays an egg a day, with an average clutch of ten to fifteen eggs. Incubation is completed in twenty-four days. In the northern regions, the peak hatching period comes in mid-June.

During incubation, hens leave the nest only for a short time, feeding at daybreak and late in the evening. As hatching time draws near, a hen seldom leaves, even if an intruder is close by. The hatch takes a few hours, and this is a critical time for the hen and her chicks. As soon as the last chick is hatched and dry, the female leads the young brood away.

The prairie chicken may renest if the first nest is destroyed or abandoned, but habitat and other requirements must be favorable. Egg numbers in the second clutch are frequently much less than the first, although survival rates in later clutches are often better, as they are hatched in better weather conditions.

After leaving the nesting area the female moves her chicks to heavier cover, where for several weeks she closely controls them, and immediately responds to their calls. Young prairie chickens face many hazards during the first few weeks of life. Wet, cold weather for long periods of time can have a profound effect on chicks, so they spend more time under the mother to stay warm and dry. In addition, for several weeks, chicks depend on insects for their main source of food; wet, cold weather reduces insect numbers, putting chicks in some jeopardy. If they survive, the young soon learn to utilize tender shoots as various greens become available. Soft seeds are also eaten when convenient.

Young chicks change rapidly. Their primary feathers start to develop, and they can fly short distances by four weeks of age. Once young birds start to fly, they become more active and feed farther away from the hen. By the sixth week, young broods travel farther to feed, moving to grainfields and open grounds.

Young chickens do not need fresh water to survive. They feed on moisture-laden greens, berries, and insects for their daily water requirements, although morning dew and water sources are frequently used if the range is dry, and lush vegetation is not available.

Unlike the sage hen, young chicks seldom mix with other families. In early fall, broods start to band together in loose flocks, with groups of adult males, females, and juveniles assembling as cold weather arrives. These large flocks do not gather just to search for food, but to survive from predators as well.

Once the adult males leave the breeding ground, they live alone, or with a small number of other males until late fall. Some males return to the lek for short periods in the fall, possibly due to the fact that day length is similar to the spring season's. Males break away from large flocks as soon as the snow leaves the booming grounds in spring, and the cycle begins again.

Late one summer, just before the opening of hunting season, I looked over several allotments (land leased from the government) for chickens in the national grasslands of South Dakota. It was extremely dry that summer, and most of the small stock dams were bone-dry and devoid of green vegetation. I ran several dogs around the empty stock dams looking for fresh chicken sign, but had no luck. Toward evening on the same day, I moved to a new location on a private holding. The sun was low on the horizon when I put three dogs down. A wide, grassy area meandered through a newly cut milo field, and extended to a large reservoir. The grassy swale was moist and green vegetation was abundant, even though it was over two miles to water. The landscape changed abruptly to a deeply eroded draw with brushy gullies feeding in from the sides. As I walked down, the cut field disappeared from above. Below, the draw had pockets of muddy water. Flash floods had cut deep into the brown soil, exposing many layers. The top layers may once have been a stream bed when the first prairie chickens moved westward to feed in the new grainfields.

The gully's low sides sparkled as a soft wind blew across the little bluestem grass choked with prairie roses and patches of wild plum. The temperature had dropped to 60 degrees by the time to the dogs reached the first side gully. The sun's presence was lost at the bottom, where a trickle of fresh water flowed. The west side was absent of sunshine as well, muting the bright fall colors.

My dogs Winston and Hershey were cooling off in a small, sandy bowl of fresh spring water when Shoe went on point facing toward the first patch of half-leaved wild plums. Suddenly, there were birds moving out the other side of the plum thicket, their wings skimming the tops of the low brush, sounding the clut-lut-lut alarm call of the sharptail. Twenty birds grasped the wind and winged over the top toward the cut stubble. There was not a chicken in the bunch. Three dogs disappeared over the horizon as my whistle sounded to no avail.

Coming back downwind, the trio charged through bluestem grass on the slope, finally responding to the fifteenth blast from the whistle. Suddenly the grassy hillside seemed to come alive with wings and rise up. The dogs had just run through the largest flock of prairie chickens I had ever seen, and that is still true to this day. Birds scattered in all directions, their wings catching the sunlight as the dogs slammed on the brakes, their eyes rolling back to watch the chickens leave. We didn't go any farther; hunting season started the next day.

FOOD SOURCES

The prairie chicken's diet consists of a wide variety of foods. Like its distant relative, the domestic chicken, this grouse eats just about every vegetable and insect within its reach. Young chicks start foraging for small insects as soon as the hen leads them away from the nest. Prairie grouse of all ages feed on insects in the spring, summer, and fall for as long as they are plentiful. Particularly fond of grasshoppers, chickens fly to meadows and open areas in search of them. I check the crop contents of every bird my guests or I shoot throughout the season. I have found hoppers that were blackened by frost in prairie grouse crops as late as the end of November.

In autumn, all kinds of foods are present, allowing chickens to become very selective in consuming their favorites, such as greens, berries, small fruit, tender buds, insects, weed seeds, and cereal grains.

One season, my wife and I spent several days hunting prairie chickens in the national grasslands. The first day we concentrated on the leeward side of a long, low ridge where grasses and forbs (broad-leafed herbs) were lush and bountiful. The day was ideal for running dogs, with a cool breeze blowing. Bobbie and I had a lot of opportunities to shoot sharptails, but few for chickens. After a couple of hours, we finally managed to collect a brace of young male prairie chickens, and called it quits for the day.

As soon as we got back to the hunting rig, I put the dogs back in their compartments, and removed the internal organs and crops of the two birds. I was cutting open the crops on the tailgate to examine them when a young game officer drove up. He walked over and introduced himself, and the three of us examined the crop contents. Ninety percent of the contents were closed yellow flowers. After close examination, we determined them to be prickly lettuce leaves and buds.

I asked the conservation officer about places I might find more chickens, and if he knew of any locations that had good stands of prickly lettuce, as the stems grow tall above most grass and are highly visible. He was extremely helpful, and pointed out several locations on the grasslands map where he thought he remembered seeing scattered prickly lettuce. Before he left, he checked our licenses and sexed the two birds. We thanked him, and returned to our motel in town.

The following day I took his advice, and went to one of the areas he pointed out. It didn't take the dogs long to find several nice flocks of prairie chickens feeding on prickly lettuce.

During winter, plenty of food is still available for prairie chickens, such as leftover agricultural crops, buds from a variety of trees, shrubs, fruits, and leftovers from livestock feeding operations. Food at this time of year is more concentrated, so the search requires traveling greater distances.

NEIGHBORS AND HAZARDS

Sharp-tailed grouse and prairie chickens not only occupy the same habitat in many areas, they also use the same breeding grounds, and occasionally hybridize. Pheasants also share some of the same country with grouse and chickens, but they mainly use grassy draws and brushy areas with more vegetation. While pheasants rarely occupy open ridges and side hills, all prairie grouse use the lower brushy areas. Conservation Reserve Program fields may also hold grouse and pheasants, so when hunting these areas be aware that all three species may be present.

In most states, prairie grouse and pheasant hunting seasons do not start at the same time, so it is important to learn the vocal sounds and flight patterns of each upland game bird in a given area. The majority of sportsmen won't shoot if they cannot identify the bird in the air, which is a good thing as it will usually be the hen pheasant the hunter confuses with the chicken.

The sound a bird hunter hears after flushing a chicken

Chickens and sharptails can occupy the same habitat in many areas, but their flight patterns, color and markings are quite different. Left, sharptail, right, prairie chicken.

is a low, soft cackle or cluck. This low cluck is very different from the call of a flushing sharp-tailed grouse. The calls of these two grouse are easy to learn, and are quite helpful in identifying the species after the flush. As a general rule, sharptail are more vocal, with a higher pitched and louder sound than chickens.

In addition to sound, flight is an easy way to distinguish the two. While both flush similarly, once airborne, a chicken's wing beats are slower, and its wings less cupped. If a chicken is viewed from the side while flying, the top of its wing appears flat, almost the same as a domestic pigeon or willow ptarmigan. From a distance, I believe these aspects are easier to distinguish than the shape of the body or tail. Also, the dark color of a chicken compared to the light color of a sharptail may be a good method of identification, although if backlit both birds appear dark.

I once invited an acquaintance to hunt for prairie grouse in South Dakota. While he had hunted a couple of years in the prairie states, most of his experience was in shooting released pheasants in his home state. As we were driving to our destination, I reminded him that the only season open was for prairie grouse and mourning doves, and that identifying sharptails and prairie chickens can be confusing, especially when they're flying in low-light conditions, or directly into the sun. I said I was going to concentrate on shooting just a chicken or two. The bag limit of three birds was for either grouse species, so for him it wouldn't make any difference. My hunting place had pheasants, but with his pheasant hunting experience, I never thought to inform him about identification of a pheasant in relation to the two grouse species.

Identifying a flying hen pheasant is relatively easy with a little practice. She is shaped like a torpedo with a long, pointed tail. In addition, pheasants rarely occupy the same type cover as prairie birds, and with a hunting dog the birds react quite differently. A pheasant regularly runs and flushes horizontal to the ground, with wing beats that are straight, not cupped. Prairie chicken and sharp-tailed grouse appear round or plump in flight, and push off vertically, frequently flushing together in small flocks.

I did mention that young pheasants were present in the area we would be hunting, so if in doubt, I told him, don't shoot. He assured me he knew what a young pheasant looked like.

To this day I don't know whether it was his inexperience, if he just didn't care, or if he had buck fever, but his identification of the birds in flight started poorly, and did not improve throughout the day. Fortunately for the young pheasants, his shooting was not the best.

It seems to me that those who hunt should take it upon themselves to learn to identify game birds in flight. It's certainly not difficult. Waterfowlers are required to learn the different ducks and geese in flight, and upland hunters should learn their birds as well.

Predators, predators everywhere. They get all the blame, and, indeed, there are many stories of various predators harassing or catching prairie grouse. Ask anyone who has spent time in the country. Ranchers, farmers, hunters, and rural mailmen all have a story or two about how they saw a falcon chasing a bunch of grouse across a plowed field, a red-tailed hawk on a post with something in its claws, or eight skunks within one mile. There are many predators that enjoy a chicken meal, but if every predator caught only upland game birds, we would no longer have game birds or predators. Probably the most destructive of the long list of culprits are the few that raid nests and eat all the eggs, but these are rarely seen.

Game birds are more aware of predators than we think. Over thousands of years of evolution and predation, game birds have adjusted their ways to avoid enemies. Using cover, flocking patterns, selection of nesting sites, flight distance, and feeding times, game birds have learned to survive.

Prairie chickens losses do occur from a variety of accidents:

nests destroyed by livestock, plowing, prairie fires, and mowing. Birds are killed along highways, flying into wires, and other obstacles. But as with other upland game birds, predation and accidents are only secondary mortality factors.

Numerous other enemies plague the chicken. Spring rains and cloudbursts turn prairies into swamps. Hail storms also destroy many nests where good cover protection is absent. Floods are always a menace, especially in low marshy areas and along river bottoms.

Drought can also be a great enemy of the chicken. When drought occurs over a long period of time, both the present and future food supply is destroyed. Lack of vegetation and shelter leaves the birds vulnerable to heat, wind, and rain. This exposure also makes them more vulnerable to predators.

The prairie grouse's total mortality is not tied to just one or two factors. Nor is the loss of prairie birds to predators, accidents, and weather significant in drastic population changes. It is the presence of suitable habitat that allows prairie chickens to stay in balance with their environment.

READING THE COVER

The prairie chicken's range has changed greatly in the last century. The never-ending prairie no longer exists. It has lost its singularity, becoming a blend of rangelands, hayfields, pastures, and reclaimed grasslands mixed with a variety of crops.

The chicken has not adapted to the changes as well as the sharptail, but it has fared at least as well, if not better, than the sage grouse. Historically, some overgrazing was an advantage for the sage grouse because it allowed sagebrush to move into grasslands, and the birds' distribution temporarily expanded. Eventually, though, loss of large sagebrush tracts brought populations down. But the prairie chicken couldn't handle overgrazing, or the spread of agriculture, and its range diminished. Today's playing field

Grasslands that support chickens must have rolling hills, knolls, ridges, and swales with different types and densities of grassy cover.

for the prairie chicken is restricted to places the plow could not cut or conquer, and to isolated areas of preserved grasslands, sandhills, and agricultural holdings. For the past two decades state and federal agencies have made great strides in rehabilitating existing parcels, and securing new lands for the recovery of good populations in many areas. South Dakota, Nebraska, and Kansas still provide good numbers for greater prairie chickens.

The basic cover types required by prairie chickens are tallgrass and mixed prairie. This does not mean that their range has to be all grassland, but at least half of it does. Like sagebrush for sage grouse, grasslands have to cover several thousand acres, and not be broken into small parcels. For this reason, much of the remaining chicken habitat is now on federal land. The government acquired these lands because they were depleted, or unwanted; some were purchased before the onslaught of settlers.

The prairie is usually the best bet to find chickens. Grasslands furnish most of the birds' daily and seasonal needs. Grasslands that support chickens must have rolling hills, knolls, ridges, and swales with different types and densities of grassy cover.

Look for uncut croplands adjacent to, or within large grasslands. These are good hangouts for chickens early in the season. After feeding early in the morning, prairie chicken flocks hit the slopes below ridges on the grasslands to loaf, chase grasshoppers, and preen themselves. Prairie chickens prefer these places for several reasons: they can look out across the prairie for danger; they can bask on the side hills that have become warm from the sun; and they can chase insects on more open slopes. These open areas also provide good dusting places. Chickens do not like to get wet, and the dew dries quickly on the sunny slopes.

I believe prairie chickens are more predictable than sharptails in their daily and seasonal movements. Reading habitat and learning the birds' daily movements are the keys to narrowing the playing field, and finding their location at different times of the day.

HUNTING TECHNIQUE

Chickens feed in grainfields early in the morning and later in the day if they are available close to grasslands. But grasslands—the larger the better—still fulfill most of the birds' daily and seasonal needs. The best time to hunt grasslands for chickens is after they feed in the morning, even though at times, and in some places their feeding place within grasslands. Look for grasslands with interesting topography, and different types and densities of grassy cover.

I seek out the highest ground first in order to view a large area, and look for the best cover available. The prairie chicken has habits similar to those of the sharptail, but is less attached to heavy, brushy cover. There is a strong correlation between time of day, and the type of cover that birds will be using.

As with sage grouse, I have a nostalgic feeling for the prairie chicken. Both are splendid game birds that once inhabited vast

The best time of day to hunt chickens in the grasslands is after they come back from feeding.

parts of North America. I first hunted sage grouse when their numbers were abundant, and later witnessed their decline. The great numbers of prairie chickens were part of a different era, and will never be the same again over a large range.

Most hunters do not think of chickens as high fliers, but I have seen them flying as high as one hundred yards. Identification at such a height can be difficult; if not observed closely, they tend to look like a flock of domestic pigeons. Early morning is the time to look for high fliers leaving their feeding grounds in the grainfields and traveling to chosen locations in the grassy cover.

If one has the opportunity, preseason scouting is certainly beneficial in shrinking the playing field. It's not foolproof, but it's time well spent. Learning where the birds are feeding, and watching their movements throughout the year can save a lot of time in locating them during the hunting season.

A UNIQUE EXPERIENCE: THE SANDHILLS

My first encounter with the Sandhills of Nebraska took place years ago. Returning home from a bobwhite quail hunting trip in Oklahoma, I was passing through, and decided to spend a day or two exploring to see what they had to offer. It was well worth the time and effort. To my amazement, the Sandhills were not a wind-blown sandy desert, but a network of grassy hills and clear lakes, streams, and reservoirs used for boating, fishing, waterfowling, and upland bird hunting. I was hooked.

The Sandhills are the largest sand dunes in the western hemisphere, and have been called the Great American Desert. They were avoided and cursed in early times by white settlers in the area. This was not country for the plow, and breaking ground was a disaster. Most of the Sandhills became cattle country, and remain so today.

During the mid-1930s, conservationists recognized the need to preserve portions of the Sandhills and its wildlife. In 1935, the Valentine National Wildlife Refuge was established as the first refuge in the area. Since then, other lands in the Sandhills have been set aside for the same purpose.

The Sandhills occupy over nineteen thousand square miles in northern Nebraska and a small portion of South Dakota. They rank as one of the largest natural grasslands in the world. Big game, upland game birds, and waterfowl are found throughout the region.

These erratic, rolling hills are held in place by grass and many other types of vegetation. The Sandhills are unusual because its flora was adopted from surrounding areas after the sands were deposited and the glaciers retreated. This phenomenon distinguishes the region from other surrounding grassland prairies.

The abundance of groundwater close to the surface creates a large number of lakes, marshes, and wetlands. The high water table also supplies rivers, small streams, and subirrigated meadows.

This, as well as annual precipitation, accounts for the vitality and abundance of plants and animals living in this beautiful region.

Grass cover is extremely fragile in the Sandhills, susceptible to a unique circumstance called wind-eroded blowouts. These blowouts start as small, disturbed places, and then expand into large, open, sandy areas devoid of most vegetation. An unusual custom used in the Sandhills for preservation of grass is placing old tires around fence posts and telephone poles to prevent a blowout from spreading around the edges. These blowouts are microenvironments within the Sandhills and contain different types of vegetation in and around the blowout fringe, such as the Hayden's or blowout penstemon, an endangered species, and blowout grass.

Sandhill hunting involves a lot of walking, and even though water is present in many places, the country is big and it is a good idea to pack a supply of water. I also recommend carrying a compass; once in the hills, everything looks the same, and a hunt for prairie grouse can take you miles from your rig.

GRASSLAND CHICKENS

I made a pledge to myself several years ago to hunt chickens at least once a year. Not because shooting a chicken is my top priority, but like sage grouse, the birds take me into a completely different environment. The beauty of the Sandhills, Flint Hills, and other windswept grasslands is unforgettable. I plan to return every year as long as I can.

Abandoned homesteads are part of the national grasslands landscape. Buildings are monuments to tillers of the soil and great windstorms. If you believe in ghosts and goblins, they're certainly present here—working on the horse-drawn sickle bar or cleaning out the grain bin for the fall harvest. Settlers toiled into the early 1930s, when severe drought and wind caused a disaster for many farmers over the Great Plains. This was the Dust Bowl of the nation. Due to this disaster, the national grasslands were born. Today, the national grasslands include thousands of acres of federal land intermixed with private farms and ranches.

Two prairie chickens flew across the road and sailed low over the long row of tangled, overgrown lilacs. The old outbuildings, gray from age and the harsh climate were collapsing, their weathered wood pulled, and taken into town to decorate new homes. The shelterbelt had grown tall and thick. The rusty windmill turned slowly, several blades missing and no longer of use. Only the foundation cornerstones stood solidly, silent witnesses to those walls where dreams were born and died.

I turned off the highway onto gravel at mile marker 26. A big, eight-wheeled tractor pulling a farm implement with high, folded wings didn't allow much room on the narrow lane. Steel shovels towered over the enclosed air-conditioned cab. A young man wearing a green and yellow hat that matched the tractor looked down and waved. Looking up, I waved back. My next turn took me down a dry, rutted lane alongside a row of galvanized steel storage bins. Harvest had been good, and was almost complete, with a large mound of silage piled in front of the overfilled bins. Following the dusty lane, I drove between enormous stubblefields cut shorter than a grasshopper's stomach.

The rancher said the chickens had been feeding in the milo while it was being cut. A mile and a half down the lane I stopped, opened the wire gate, and entered the Taylor Allotment, four sections of land that were being rested that year. I closed the gate and parked the hunting rig. There were no traces of tire tracks after last week's rain.

I would be hunting alone for the next three hours, as my two hunting partners would not arrive until after lunch. Having hunted the two previous days with a couple of local sportsmen from South Dakota, I looked at the high distant ridge, and thought about how they would hunt the place if they were with me today.

Pointing dogs are great on prairie chickens. Early season chickens hold well, and when they are flushed, big-running pointers can relocate them quickly. Flushing and retrieving dogs are also great for hunting chickens, but the hunter has to cover more ground himself. Chicken hunting with dogs becomes more difficult as the hunting season draws to a close. This is because chickens have flocked together, and the cover has been knocked down from early snows. Dogs just cannot work the birds effectively.

New country is always a challenge, and I had the whole place to myself. A large uncut milo field was off to the left of the distant ridge a quarter mile away, and the dark brown tassels glistened in the sunlight. It was past nine when I let the dogs out of their compartments to stretch.

I slid the shotgun, a light little 28-gauge side-by-side, out of the leather case. When it came to prairie grouse hunting, I'd bagged my share with larger gauges, but I was no longer interested in shooting a lot of grouse. If I had just one shot I'd probably choose a 12-gauge with a modified choke and one ounce of No. 6 shot, but I still prefer my light gun for walking long distances.

I was putting the last handful of shells in my vest when a dozen prairie chickens skimmed over the dark milo field, flying toward the high ridge. They faded into the hills without changing direction. That bit of luck had shrunk the playing field considerably.

I put beeper collars on Shoe, Winston, Clyde, and Lewis and headed for the grasslands next to the milo field. My plan was to walk the edge of the grasslands along the milo field toward a distant ridge.

I headed toward the milo, walking through a large area of western wheatgrass mixed with an endless array of prairie forbs. The combination of grasses and forbs on the prairie is never the same from season to season or from place to place. I reasoned the grouse wouldn't be in the tall stands of grass at that time of day.

The four dogs were almost to the fence line and on their way to the private milo field when they responded to my whistle and turned toward the grassy hills. My thoughts turned to the chickens I had seen when I was dropping shells on the ground and how my local friends would have approached them. My best bet was to head in the same direction the four dogs had gone, across the rolling hills to the large ridge. Some slopes were steep and covered with little bluestem grass, while others were long and gradual with green needlegrass and side-oats grama.

Colorful forbs are always present among the grasses on the prairie, and during autumn their blooms add a variety of character to the landscape. That morning, the side hills and ridges were a palette of soft, subtle, pastel colors.

Knowing that birds tend to hole up at midday, resting in scattered patches of thin cover, I walked up a low hill with a grassy swale on each side. Forty-five minutes had passed since I last saw the chickens. I wasn't sure, but it seemed like the place the birds had landed. As the sun warmed the hillside, the dogs checked in for water several times. A rusty stock tank was off to one side, deep in the grassy swale. It looked dry, but my water jug was almost empty, so I decided to check it out.

Old Shoe came along. As I started walking down he was above me, but just below the ridge. The other three dogs were out of sight on the far side of the ridge.

Thirty yards ahead, working the gradual slope, the old dog suddenly became birdy, making a solid point into the light breeze drifting down from the ridge. I wondered if the chickens had moved over the top and been pinned by the other Brittanys.

Before I could move two birds, dark against the hill, flew over the ridge. Shoe never moved. Short of breath, I scurried up the hill toward the dog just as the herd of Brittanys came charging over the ridge chasing a single chicken, to my chagrin. Shoe still didn't move, and the gang of three slammed on their brakes and honored his point. I walked slowly toward the dogs and passed in front of

Shoe. Half a dozen birds pushed out of the golden-red cover, swung past, and sailed down the ravine toward the stock tank. I got lucky and dumped the last bird. It bounced down the hill and landed in the tall grass. Winston dove into the grass and retrieved the chicken.

The other birds scattered, landing about one hundred yards across the ravine above the tank. The golden-red grass was identical to the cover from which the first flush was made. The dogs followed the birds and pointed before I arrived. The bunch got up again—first two, then three—but I didn't fire.

I field dressed the rooster chicken by a little puddle of muddy water next to the leaking rusty tank, with the four wet dogs impatient to get going.

RING-NECKED PHEASANT
Foothill Pheasants

Pheasants that live in the foothills of mountains prefer to run uphill when pursued. These long-legged track stars can cover a lot of ground, whether horizontal or vertical. And in this country it's critical to get them to stop and hold. So one should hunt the creek bottoms first, pushing the birds into the side draws that lead to the benchland wheatfields above. As the draws peter out, and once pushed out of the good cover, these speedsters will flush and fly back towards the creek. That's when wingshooting becomes fast and furious.

I use pointing dogs to hunt pheasants, although that's not because I think they are the best match for these speedsters. Pointing dogs just happen to be my preference for hunting all

Foothill pheasants have a different playbook than their flatland cousins.

upland game birds in North America. The fact is, if the wily ring-neck pheasant was the only upland bird I hunted my choice for a canine companion would be one of the retriever breeds. But no matter how one pursues them, foothill pheasants just don't behave like their flatland cousins.

ORIGINS

The Asiatic pheasant was not the first foreign game bird introduced in North America, but it proved the most adaptable, and therefore the most successful, over a large area. In 1881 the first successful planting of ring-necked pheasant occurred in the Willamette Valley in Oregon. The birds did so well that another large shipment was released two years later. Several years after that a successful stocking occurred in New Jersey, although it paled in comparison to the western planting program. After the Willamette Valley pheasant population exploded it wasn't long before more private individuals and state game departments got involved in releasing pheasants across the nation. A large number of these projects were doomed from the beginning because of a lack of knowledge about wildlife ecology. However, many state game agencies eventually established thriving wild pheasant populations. But it soon became apparent that the northern grain belt of the nation was the area best suited for stable pheasant populations. It's pretty certain that today most of the country that can hold pheasants already do.

Over the years, the decline of once well-established pheasant strongholds is due to a growing human population, and the destruction of the birds' cover. Urban sprawl and some clean farming practices have taken a large toll on pheasant density through the years. But in the breadbasket states, where agriculture is the main commodity, and marginal croplands have returned to grasslands through the Conservation Reserve Program (CRP), pheasant populations have continued to thrive.

DISTRIBUTION

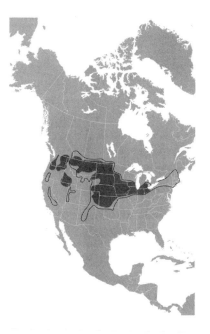

At one time, the wild pheasant's range included most of our northern states and the southern edge of Canada. But today much of the bird's habitat has been depleted by human development. Hunting clubs and preserves have sprung up in many areas to give the wingshooter some type of shooting experience. Most of these places use liberated or released birds, and though enjoyable this type of shooting won't ever replace hunting wild pheasants. The good news is that there are still thousands of acres open to the public with excellent wild pheasant hunting.

The pheasant is a bird of open farmlands and cannot survive in a total forest setting. The wide swath between the 38th and 52nd parallels in the farmland district of North America is the best zone in which to find wild pheasant. Today the most dependable hunting begins in the Midwestern states, starting with portions of Wisconsin and Minnesota and continuing down through Iowa, northern Illinois, northern Missouri, western Kansas, Nebraska, North and South Dakota, and scattered areas throughout the northwestern states all the way to the Pacific coast.

KNOWING THE BIRD

The pheasant (*Phasianus colchicus*) is easily the most popular game bird in the U.S., although whether or not it is the most hunted "wild" game bird is debatable. But wild or liberated it is still a wonderful and exciting bird to pursue. Its two most common names, ringneck or ring-necked pheasant, are derived from the bird's white neckband. The bird we know is a mixture of races descended from the Caucasian strain of western Asia.

Adult cocks range in size from thirty to thirty-six inches in length. Unlike other game birds, the tail accounts for almost two-thirds of the total length. Wingspan stretches thirty-two to thirty-four inches, and average weight runs two and a half to three and a half pounds. Adult hens range in length from twenty to twenty-five inches, with a wingspan of twenty-four to twenty-nine inches, and a weight between two and two and a quarter pounds.

In the eyes of many upland bird hunters, the adult male pheasant is the most handsome of our game birds. It is certainly a magnificent, brilliantly plumed bird. The cock has ear tufts, and bright red cheek patches around its eyes that form wattles around much of the head. The beak is bluish-white and chicken-like. The

Pheasant prefer to run under most conditions.

rest of the head and neck are iridescent green, separated from the body by a white collar. The body is colorful, with many rich, metallic, bronze, brown-red, black, and gray markings. The long pointed tail is light brown with dark bars. The legs lack feathers but have spurs.

The hen is smaller in size, and her coloration includes several shades of mottled light browns, with dark markings throughout her body. Unlike the male, she does not have a white ring around her neck. The female has a pointed, light-brown, barred tail, although it's shorter than her partner's. The hen's legs are bare and lack spurs.

In flight the brightly colored male appears much darker than the female. Other features of the cock are the white collar around its neck and long dark tail. The male will often utter a coarse cackle when flying (*cuct-et cuct-et cuct-cuct*), while the hens are mostly silent. They can make a high-pitched sound (*queep-queep*), but this is not a sure method of identification. Following a pheasant into the sun, or in low light can make it difficult to distinguish between the sexes. When in doubt, don't shoot.

Pheasants would rather run than fly, but are still strong fliers for short flights. Once flushed, they have an explosive takeoff that usually occurs in any direction except the one you are expecting. The rounded wings are built for sudden power strokes, and are short in comparison to body size. Pheasants can hit speeds topping thirty-five miles per hour in just a matter of seconds, but they also glide a lot to conserve energy. Many cock birds will fly and glide over three-quarters of a mile before landing. Flight distance depends on the cover the bird is looking for as an escape route.

LIFE CYCLE

Once the males' territorial confrontations are over, only a single rooster occupies a given "property." Crowing is the rooster's way of showing other males that the location is taken. Usually the crowing area is along open edges of fields and woody cover. Mating takes place at least a month after the male courtship activities, and by then the rooster may have collected several other females that have chosen his territory for nesting.

The hen pheasant's primary nesting cover is grass, but similar covers are used. Places like irrigation ditches, roadside ditches, edges of shelterbelts, corners of crop fields, and fence rows all are utilized. Pastures, woodlots, and tilled fields don't provide adequate nesting cover, and just don't seem conducive to the female's requirements. The lack of good nesting habitat is one of the major reasons some areas are void of game birds.

In most areas egg-laying starts in mid- to late April and may continue into summer, especially if a nest is destroyed. Most hens will renest if they lose their first clutch. The average clutch size is eight to twelve eggs, and it takes about two weeks for the hen to lay this number. Incubation takes roughly another twenty-four days. So it generally takes about five total weeks from the start of laying for the young to hatch. Seeing different sizes and age groups doesn't indicate that a single hen had more than one brood; rather, it only means she renested after losing her first or second clutch.

The CRP fields have contributed greatly to higher nesting success, and are certainly responsible for population increases. Pheasant populations reach their highest point during the summer brood season, and the lowest during the breeding season. The fact is, only about 30 percent of young pheasants survive to the following spring, sometimes less. A two-year-old pheasant is comparatively old.

Pheasant numbers are affected by diversity of cover crops, weather, seasonal changes, and long-term land practices. The quantity and quality of the habitat is the determining factor in maintaining a carrying capacity for any species. Without the habitat requirements the species eventually dies out.

The first broods begin hatching in mid-May. And this is by far the most successful period for good numbers hatched. As the spring season progresses, the success rate declines. Once the last chick hatches, the female leads them all away from the nest. The female rears the brood. Although the male doesn't actually stay with his families, he does play a role in guarding the broods he has fathered from intruders. As with all upland game birds, in the first couple of weeks the chicks are very reclusive and never flush. Their best tactic is simply to freeze. But after two weeks the young chicks can run and fly, and they begin to use the best escape route to get away.

The brood spends most of the summer in its nesting territory. At first the chicks' diet is mostly insects, but as the young birds grow they add many other edible seeds, fruits, and greens. Young pheasants are notorious for eating anything that moves or grows and fits in their small beaks.

As summer advances, the birds become strong fliers and are more mobile and less dependent on their brood territory, especially if food becomes scarce. If food is still available their range expands very little. The family group stays together most of the summer, but as the youngsters grow they begin to show their independence, and the family brood starts to break up into a looser group.

As autumn approaches, their summer range may become less adequate, and the birds may be forced to shift to new feeding areas. Crops are harvested, hayfields cut, and the birds' whole habitat may change. Movement is the only way to survive. At this time family groups join up with one another to form larger loose flocks.

Instead of being spread more or less evenly over a large range like many other game birds, during fall and winter pheasants tend to concentrate in more restricted cover that suits all their needs. It is not unusual for young pheasants to travel several miles from their summer cover to reach good habitat. Birds often visit grain bins, feedlots, and shelterbelts where food is available on a daily basis. In some areas bird will move down in elevation to valleys or marshy areas with heavy cover.

Pheasants prefer to run under most conditions, but if pushed out of good cover they will flush. By late fall, young pheasants are strong fliers although they cannot sustain extended flights.

In autumn young birds have reached adult size, and the broods have broken up for pre-winter conditioning. Pheasant are in mixed sexes, singles, and small flocks in late fall. In good years of high pheasant population, large flocks of forty or more birds will choose to remain in protective cover close to food sources.

Winter is the critical period for pheasants, and great losses can occur during severe winters. It's important for pheasants to have heavy protective cover and adequate winter food in order to maintain a solid breeding population to begin the cycle again. It takes a pretty harsh weather to really cause heavy mortality if food and good shelter are available. Several years ago a severe winter storm dumped deep, heavy snow across a wide swath of good pheasant country along the northern tier of the High Plains. Some efforts were made to feed birds, but that only happened in a few places where access was easy. This would be like fertilizing one inch of a football field and hoping the whole playing area would green up. There were reports that many areas had high mortality, but where well-established heavy overhead shelter and native foods were available the birds did quite well. That's why the more "edges" a pheasant lives around, the more likely it is to survive.

FOOD SOURCES

When the mother leads her brood off the nest the chicks quickly learn to feed on small insects that are high in protein for needed growth. After several weeks the young birds add a wide variety of insects and tender greens to their diet. As the season progresses wheat, barley, oats, corn, beans, peas, sorghum, weed seeds, grasses, wild oats, thistle seeds, sunflower seeds, fruits, dandelions, sweet clover, insects, snails, and many other plants and animals are readily consumed. As winter approaches, the diet of juveniles and adults is mostly cereal grains due to their availability. But when food becomes scarce pheasants will eat almost anything. They also consume small rocks (grit) to aid in grinding their food.

Pheasants obtain water in many forms, such as insects, fruits, green vegetation, rain, dew, and snow. Open water like ponds, creeks, and ditches are useful, but not necessary. Wetlands are utilized by pheasants, but mostly for protection.

Pheasants normally roost on the ground in grassy cover, leave at daybreak, and begin feeding at sunrise. During overcast days or bad morning weather, they change their feeding habits. Like most wildlife, if there is a change in weather or a front approaching, the pheasant will feed longer to take advantage of the light. Daybreak and sunset are excellent times to drive the gravel roads and spot the birds for the next day's hunt. In the early part of the morning, the birds typically are feeding and moving around.

Once pheasants are full of food and have gathered enough grit they seek denser cover along waterways and draws, preferably with a canopy of willows, rosebushes, or other higher vegetation. In the middle of the day, birds may move to dusting areas for short periods, and occasionally they lie out in the open and sun themselves on cool days. Later in the day, the birds begin moving to feeding grounds and grit spots before returning to their roosting places in CRP fields, grassy draws, or other suitable cover. In cold weather, pheasants roost in cattails and other dense cover.

NEIGHBORS AND HAZARDS

Early in the season juvenile hen pheasants can be confused with young sharp-tailed grouse and prairie chickens. In flight, a young pheasant appears light brown in color, has a longer body profile, and has a pointed light-brown tail. A sharptail on the wing looks white in color, and has a plump body with a light-colored pointed tail. Whereas a prairie chicken, when flushed, appears darker brown with a plump body and a dark round tail. All three species have different vocal sounds, wing beats, and flight patterns. With a little effort, it is easy to identify these characteristics.

Like all game birds, pheasants are subject to periods of population fluctuation from many causes, including predation. But also like all gallinaceous birds, pheasants are such prolific breeders that enemies do not seriously reduce their numbers. While many think predation is a major factor, it is not. Predation is most common during nesting, lessens as chicks develop, and is infrequent with adult birds. Aerial and ground predators do play a small part in pheasant mortality, but it is the type and amount of cover that determines predation levels—sparse cover makes for easy pickings.

While training dogs one August, I observed through my binoculars a red fox with pups by their den along a creek bottom.

The willows were high and the cover heavy. Around the den was a large mound of open grassland about thirty yards square. The young pheasants would go out into the grass and chase grasshoppers, paying little attention to the vixen and the pups rolling around in the dirt and chasing one another. After a time, the female got up and stretched her front feet forward and yawned, sending the pheasants back into the cover. I approached the site with my dogs, putting the fox family down the hole and the pheasants on the run for heavy cover. The dogs pointed several birds, but most of the pheasants funneled down the creek through the heavy cover. I returned to the den and examined the bones and fox scat around the site. I did find a number of pheasant bones, but to my surprise most of the debris included rodent bones, grasshopper wings, fruits, seeds, and other vegetation I could not identify. The habitat was excellent, and provided the young birds with good escape routes. That fall the pheasant hunting on that particular stretch of creek bottom was outstanding. The combination of different vegetation cover in an area is the key to good pheasant populations and pheasant hunting.

READING THE COVER

For the local hunter, scouting is an effective way to find birds before the hunting season starts, but it's not feasible for the traveling wingshooter on a long trip. So it's essential to be able to read pheasant cover, and learn how a bird spends it day no matter where you go to hunt. This saves valuable time in the field, which is critical on any hunting trip.

Food, lots of different levels of cover, and a water source are the basic requirements for wild pheasants everywhere. Learning how pheasants use these combinations will translate into a successful hunt. So when talking about locating good pheasant cover we are generally referring to feeding, breeding, nesting, roosting, escape, travel, and winter cover. The water source requirement is one of the most flexible because birds can also obtain water from succulent greens, fruits, and insects, or rain drops. Like all game birds, pheasants have different seasonal activities.

I look at habitat as a place where an animal or plant naturally lives or grows. I think of cover as protection and shelter for an animal. Ideal pheasant country has to have good habitat and good cover. This combination is the balance between uncultivated land and cultivated land, and the more edges the better.

Large blocks of dryland farming provide a food source for pheasants, but lack cover for protection. The same holds true for large areas of shrub grasslands and plains grassland, but in reverse—cover, but no food. Diversity of cover types and food crops perform a variety of functions for pheasants. Trees, shrubs, woody plants, and thorny bushes mostly associated with a waterway provide the pheasant with shade and protection from wind, sun, and predators all year long. Undisturbed vegetation such as CRP fields (land taken out of agricultural production and planted to permanent cover), fence lines, and road rights-of-way provides nesting and brood cover. Wetlands, cattail marshes, weedy patches, and brushy draws are used for loafing, dusting, and roosting. Edges of fields, fence rows, ditches, narrow draws running into grainfields, and roadsides provide travel lanes for food or escape.

When locating hunting areas for pheasants look for diversity of cover types plus croplands: major riparian bottomlands and their tributaries, large irrigated water impoundments with adjacent croplands, dryland farming areas interrupted by brushy draws, and steep grassy slopes, marshes, CRP tracts, and other terrain unsuitable for tillage yet bordered by agriculture cropland.

Pheasants leave a lot of sign in places they congregate. Their droppings are chicken-like, and easily distinguished. Favorite loafing places will have feathers, dropping, and well-defined dusting bowls. Pheasants also disturb large areas by scratching the ground to uncover food, a good visible sign that birds are close by.

HUNTING TECHNIQUE

The methods used in hunting pheasants are possibly as numerous as pheasant hunters. First, learn the bird's feeding habits, preferred habitats, and hunting areas, all of which are discussed above. Whether hunting with or without dogs, try to head out early in the morning and hunt the edges of grainfields and old homesteads adjacent to crops. Walk draws running into croplands, high-cut stubblefields close to vegetation areas, cover along fence rows with feed, and around reservoirs and stock ponds located near food sources. These are the places where birds can feed yet still have escape routes.

Getting enough grain and grit may take pheasants only an hour or so. After feeding, pheasants will move into CRP tracts, high canopy areas, and tall weedy hangouts. At midday, hunt the CRP fields, creek bottoms, large draws, and woody thickets. Late in the afternoon, birds will be moving to feeding areas so hunt

The methods used in hunting pheasants are possibly as numerous as pheasant hunters.

the same cover you did in the morning. Working extremely heavy cover such as cattails can be productive, but it's usually better later in the season when hunting pressure and cold weather are larger factors.

Hunting large CRP fields or croplands alone may be futile, but hunting the same area with dogs often nets outstanding results. Two or more hunters can walk the fields from opposite ends, cutting the edges of the field. This prevents pheasants from running out. Move along in a zigzag pattern and stop often to give the pheasants a chance to flush. When walking in large fields with several hunters, lines should be staggered, not straight. Pheasants often circle around the hunters and are pushed into the trailing person. When hunting creek bottoms and long draws it can be effective to have two or more hunters act as blockers, with or without dogs. Meandering creeks, oxbows, and turns can provide a place to cut off birds. Isolated patches of cover should

What kind of dog makes the best pheasant dog? The kind that hunts close and likes to retrieve birds.

be approached from two sides. The important thing about this maneuver is that all hunters know everyone's location. Safety is particularly important in such situations.

So what kind of dog makes the best pheasant dog? The kind that hunts close and likes to retrieve birds. I believe flushing and retrieving dogs are the best all-around pheasant dogs. If trained properly, a dog working back and forth in front of the hunter within twenty-five yards is deadly on running pheasant. It takes a very smart pheasant to escape a good flushing dog.

Pointing breeds that work close or trail are worthwhile pheasant dogs, but I admit, my big-running pointing dogs are only fair pheasant dogs. Fast-moving pointing dogs occasionally pin down pheasants, but most good pointers have a lot of trouble with them. While the dog is on point, the pheasant runs out. Conversely, many good pointing dogs that have been worked on running pheasants will overreact to other game birds, pushing them too much and flushing them.

One of my favorite ways to hunt pheasants is to work the creek bottoms with my older dogs, moving the birds ahead or forcing them into the small side draws that many lead to the upper benchlands. Later, I slowly hunt the small draws, pushing the pheasants ahead. As the draws tighten some of the birds will stop and hold for the dogs. That's when all heck breaks loose.

After shooting a pheasant, the first responsibility is to find the bird. Any well-trained bird dog, whatever the breed, will save the hunter many downed and crippled birds. I once hunted with a man who, to my chagrin, insisted on bringing his female German shepherd. She walked ahead of her master, never bothering my pointers. The big female was polite and did not mind my dogs retrieving the birds they found first. Sven was sure she found and retrieved most of the downed birds that day.

When I hunt pheasants my 5 3/4-pound, 16-gauge side-by-side with improved cylinder and modified works best, whether it's early or late in the season. Over dogs and for all-around use on pheasants No. 6 shot is my favorite.

I believe a 12-gauge might be better, but I have always used a light, fast shotgun. I know the capabilities of my sweet 16-gauge and deliberately avoid long, iffy shots. Big guns may be the most popular, but I still think a gun is more of a personal choice.

THINGS I'VE LEARNED

I've always had this notion about hunting time being paramount in my daily schedule. Dogs, game birds, and guns have always been in the forefront of my thinking. As a teenager, my desire for work went no farther than affording a shotgun so I could take my untrained springer spaniel on a real bird hunt. I marked each day on the calendar and calculated the number of newspapers to be delivered after school before I had enough money to buy the shotgun and a box of shells.

Now that was around 1946 and you could buy a Stevens single-barreled shotgun and a box of shells for about twenty-five bucks and some change, plus shipping. I've always had a high regard for work ethics, but long hours at work and long periods of continuous sporting endeavors don't always fit together unless both are in the same neighborhood.

When the time came I chose a couple of professions that allowed me more time in the field without jeopardizing my work principles. But the most important element is having a place to play just beyond the window from where you work. And back then, finding a job that fit the bill yet paid a living wage was a real challenge.

I'm afraid that if I had not chosen to come west when I did, if I had taken a job in a large city or tried to become rich—something we've all wished for from time to time—it would have taken a lot of fun out of my hunting pursuits. For instance, if I had joined a prestigious hunting club near an urban center I doubt if I ever would have really appreciated walking for untold miles across the open prairie in search of game birds that local folks said could not be hunted. To hunt this way, I've worn out more shoe leather than it takes to build a western saddle. But the time I put in traversing the countryside made shooting one or two wild Huns considerably more valuable to me, the same way ice fishing was always more fun if you skipped school to do it.

I've known some folks who hunted hard during their working lives, and then upon retirement moved to a location surrounded by pay-to-go hunting preserves teeming with pheasants, only to lose interest in the sport when it seemed too easy. I guess they figured they had accomplished the ultimate in bird hunting. Maybe they hadn't figured it out; it really was too easy. Travel, inconvenience, effort, and sometimes being unsuccessful are part of the fun. There are times when it takes a lot of hassle to make a good hunt.

A long time ago, I spent some time during an upland bird season hunting pheasants. Back then you could hunt anywhere; it was just a matter of getting in your rig and going. Not that pheasants topped my list of favorite game birds even then, but my hunting partner at the time had always been crazy about long-tailed roosters.

We'd swap weekends driving our look-alike Volkswagens in pursuit of pheasant hunting haunts. We were still at that age when driving in bad weather and on awful roads never bothered us. The fact is, both of us looked upon severe weather conditions as the best time to hunt pheasants. "The colder, the better," became our motto.

I supplied the dogs and he the lunches. Gasoline was reasonable, mom and pop motels cheap, and cafés with checkered oilcloth table settings the norm. These trips were hardcore hunting adventures rather than recreational jaunts, or something a spouse might enjoy.

It's cold enough that the defroster doesn't completely clear the frost off the front widow. Six inches of new snow lies on the ground, and temperatures are still falling below zero. I park the car and we step out into the cold, crystal-clear air. With every movement the snow squeaks underfoot. The two Brittanys don't seem to mind the cold weather. They pace back and forth, kicking up powder, and encouraging us to hurry. Hoarfrost covers the dogs' eyelids and muzzles by the time we get going.

I slide down the incline, slowly gaining speed until the cattails stop my fall at the edge of the long slough. The two dogs never hesitate. They cross the cattail island, and are out of sight before I regain my footing. My next steps are worse. A covering of snow over thin ice gives way beneath both feet. Icy water leaks over the tops of my insulated pacs, instantly freezing my canvas trousers.

My partner is slowly plowing through the cattails farther down the slough, apparently walking on hard ice. He waves me on just as a horde of pheasants pile out the far end of the cattails with the two dogs in hot pursuit.

"I hate pheasants and where they live!" I yell as I head for the Volkswagen to warm up.

After some time, the floor heater starts to put out delightfully warm air. I partly dry the pacs and thaw out the bottoms of my trousers. Trying to put socks and pacs on under wet hunting pants while sitting in the front seat of a VW Bug is like trying to get coveralls on in the back seat of a Super Cub. It can't be done efficiently, so I just hang out the front door of the Bug and pull on a clean, dry wool sock over a cold, wet foot and then lace up the pac. This accomplished, I stand and balance on one foot as best I can while struggling into the other sock and boot. This is quite a trick in deep snow when it's below zero.

Shortly after I finish the sock-hop my hunting partner returns. "What are you doing back at the hunting rig?" he says with a half grin. Looking down at my stiff trousers and frozen pacs, he innocently asks, "What happened?" As if he didn't know.

"A little snow covered the warm spring channel and I stepped right through into a foot of water," I explained, to further laughter.

"Did you see all the roosters blow out the end of the cattails? Both dogs pointed rock solid, but the birds didn't hold. There must have been fifty of them. Let's go get 'em," he said, pointing toward the deep valley and brushy breaks descending from the wheatfields above to the meandering river below.

"Yeah," I said, continuously knocking both feet together to keep the blood circulating, "hiking up and down the steep draws full of buffalo berry brush after running pheasants may help to keep my feet warm. Anyway, it will keep them from freezing. Let's go. The dogs are getting impatient."

We head toward where he had first crossed the frozen cattail slough. He and the dogs are in high spirits, leading the charge to where the pheasants went.

After a hard day's hunt, my feet are still feeling wet, but warm. We both managed to kill a couple of roosters, still short of our limit. Halfway to the motel the Volkswagen's heater finally warms us up. The cold-nosed dogs lie curled up in the back seat, exhausted.

Recently, I just happened to be in the area. It was early afternoon when I stopped to hunt the same place at about the same time of year. I parked my pickup over the long-gone tracks of the Volkswagen. I put three dogs down, one a pointer and two Brittanys, and slowly angled down the incline. It was shirtsleeve weather and much too warm for pheasant hunting. The slough no longer carried spring-fed water and smooth brome grass has replaced the cattails except at the far end. The cattails had been reduced in size to a small triangular patch about thirty feet wide. All three dogs froze at the edge of the cattails, waiting for me to arrive. The young pointer broke first, followed by the Brittanys. The cattails vibrated as the dogs plowed through the heavy cover, sending bursts of catkins aloft. It was over in seconds. Two single roosters flushed moments apart, and I put both of them down. I slowly removed the empty hulls from the 16-gauge side-by-side and watched five more big roosters feather the wind and sail towards the river breaks. Two birds were enough, and I headed for the hunting rig. The pickup was still warm when I got in the cab.

Driving out, I remembered the long-ago hunt in freezing weather, my wet, cold feet on the long walk, the hordes of pheasant lifting out of the slough, the cramped hunting rig, and the two happy hard-working dogs curled up in the back seat. This hunt was too easy, I thought. I guess it really was more fun chasing pheasants up and down the breaks on cold feet and having bone-tired dogs at day's end. One thing I've recently learned, you have to work at it.

WESTERN RUFFED GROUSE

A Gentleman's Bird

At one time the eastern ruffed grouse was one of several game species that the early settler depended on to help feed his pioneering family. During this period there was little sport in ruffed grouse hunting, and the bird was considered the fool hen of the forest. As agriculture bloomed and cities grew, the harvest of grouse became a commercial enterprise. Market hunting flourished for most of a century, and this eventually changed the bird from a branch-sitting target to a quick-flushing quarry. With the advent of more restrictive hunting laws, pursuing this now-wily game bird became a gentleman's field sport.

Today there are two kinds of ruffed grouse hunting: traditional hunting and western hunting.

There are two times to hunt ruffed grouse in the West: during the green season, and when the landscape is ablaze with hues of smoky gold and rusty red. Generally, western ruffed grouse are birds of forest succession. They live in the foothills and lower mountain elevations where patches of hardwood mix with the coniferous forest near moist seeps or watercourses. Like their eastern cousins, western ruffed grouse like edges where different cover types come together. And unlike most other western game birds of the open spaces, a ruff's living space is thought of in acres. Ruffed grouse stay put in the low-lying areas of aspen groves and mixed forest types year-round, and only expand their cruising range for a new food source.

The western ruffed grouse of today still acts much like its eastern cousin of a century ago, but no matter where you hunt them they should still be treated as the same fine gentleman's game bird.

ORIGINS

Ruffed grouse are native to the northern forests of North America, and were there long before any humans arrived on the scene. Fossil evidence suggests that they lived here during the interglacial periods, and probably have been present for half a million years. Natural ecological forest succession, from wind and fire, have kept these forests young through the centuries, allowing thousands of generations of ruffed grouse to sustain a living population.

DISTRIBUTION

Ruffed grouse are found in woodland regions from the Atlantic to the Pacific, from Alaska down through the Coastal Mountains and Rocky Mountains, from Hudson's Bay through the Great Lakes states, and from Labrador down to the southern Appalachians. But their distribution within this vast forest region is more closely related to immature woodland fringes than the mature stands of forest habitat.

KNOWING THE BIRD

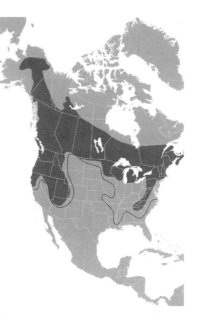

The bird's accepted name across North America is ruffed grouse; however, the first name given it by early eastern settlers was probably "fool hen" or "wood hen." Later, as the ruffed grouse became more of a sporting prize, the name "partridge" or "pa'tridge" came into use. In Appalachian country hunters referred to them as "mountain pheasant." Although names like partridge and pheasant were widely used, the bird is neither a partridge nor a true pheasant. In the mountainous West the most common name was once "wood chicken."

The ruffed grouse (*Bonasa umbellus*) is the sole member of its genus in North America, but it is closely related to the hazel hen (*Bonasa sylvestris*) of Europe. The bird's scientific name comes from the Latin word for bison, as in a grouse drumming is like a bison bellowing. The species name *umbellus* refers to an umbrella, and is descriptive of the bird's feather tufts, or ruffs on the neck.

I lay no claim to being an authority on the bird's taxonomy, and there is still some question of the number of subspecies of ruffed grouse that exist today. At this time, the American Ornithologist Union recognizes seven subspecies or races of ruffed grouse that live in North America. This book deals with the subspecies that live in northwestern North America, which I will simply call western ruffed grouse or ruffed grouse.

Ruffed grouse are a sportsman's prize.

The ruffed grouse exhibits a wide variation in color, and each subspecies has its own color variations, from dark grays to light grays, and from dark browns to light browns. Interestingly, not all of the subspecies come in the two distinct gray and brown color phases, and there are really a multitude of color phases that show up regionally.

Ruffed grouse run between fifteen and nineteen inches long, have a wingspan of twenty-three to twenty-five inches, and weigh about a pound and a half to two pounds, which makes them appear rather plump. When flushed, a distinct tail of five to eight inches long becomes quite evident. Most subspecies are predominantly of the brown phase, although birds of the Northwest and in higher elevations are often mostly gray.

The head, back, and upper parts of the body are gray-brown, brown, black, and white, with oval spots. The feathers on top of the head lie back, and make a crest when raised. The bird has a buff chin patch and a light line under its eye. Ruffed grouse have a collar, or ruff, of feathers around their neck, which gives the bird its name. The upper parts of the body have mottled white and black markings that vary greatly among individual birds. On the lower body the background color is light gray, broken by bars of blackish browns and grays. Ruffed grouse have a long fan-shaped tail with narrow bands of blackish brown and one wide band at the end of the tail. The side and breast are light gray with large dark bars on its side, fading narrow lines run through the breast. The legs are feathered to the toes. In winter grouse grow outgrowths, or snowshoes along the edges of the toes to aid in walking on deep snow.

The sexes are similar, but adult males are usually larger and heavier than females. Females also have a shorter tail, and their dark band is not continuous around the base of the tail. In hand, the best identification between the sexes is the markings on the rump tail feathers. The female has only one white dot on each feather, whereas the male has two or more dots.

Ruffed grouse make a thunderous roar of wing beats when flushing off the ground, or sometimes from trees. In flight, the bars are prominent, with the long dark fanned tail making their identification fairly easy. Adult males will usually climb steeply, while the adult female will fly lower to the ground. Ruffed grouse do not fly exceptionally fast, but this can be very deceptive because of the twists and turns they make to dodge brush and trees at close range. Once flushed, western ruffs will quickly try to get some object between themselves and you—unless they haven't been hunted much, in which case they may just flutter up to the nearest tree branch and stare down at you.

LIFE CYCLE

Ruffed grouse are nonmigratory, and tend to spend their entire lives within a small area. It is probably safe to say that most birds live out their short life span of two to four years within a mile of where they were hatched.

The male ruffed grouse is a rather solitary bird most of the year, with the exception being during the spring breeding season. At this time the male spends a lot of time trying to attract females by drumming loudly while standing on a fallen log. The hen mates but once during the season. She then selects a nest site within a half mile of where she was bred. She incubates her eggs and rears the brood without any assistance from the male.

The nest is usually located against a stump, clump, or tree to give the hen protection from the back. Her camouflaged colors blend into the material of the nest, and at times she may even put a few leaves over her back for better concealment. She lays eight to twelve eggs over a period of about fifteen days, and spends twenty-two days incubating them. A hen will sometimes renest if she loses the first clutch of eggs early in the nesting cycle. But there is not enough time during the summer months for a female grouse to bring off two broods in a year.

Young grouse resemble a charred marshmallow when hatched. The mother leaves the nest as soon as the last egg has hatched to get her brood into open areas where more insects are available. The hen can spot danger quickly, calling her chicks to scatter and freeze while she uses the broken wing trick to distract the intruder. Within a few days the young birds are able to roost in low tree branches, which offer much greater protection than the ground. Not long after that the young birds can make short flights when danger appears.

After hatching, the ruffed grouse brood will stay together until early fall. Normally no more than half of the brood will survive the summer; and even then fully-grown ruffed grouse don't last long under natural conditions. Poor habitat and weather conditions contribute greatly to the loss of young birds, with other factors only playing a small part. Population levels vary according to the carrying capacity of the habitat. Mortality from all causes varies between 40 percent and 60 percent within the yearly cycle. The birds cannot increase in number for many years in succession before a reversal occurs.

During September, often after a storm, grouse may go through a fall shuffle for some unknown reason. There are many theories as to why grouse go through this crazy phenomenon, but nothing has been proven definitively. Grouse do a lot of walking during this period, intermixed with short flights. There is evidence that after the fall shuffle grouse will regroup in loose winter flocks of roughly three to eight birds. Ruffed grouse can range over a large area if poor-quality habitat occurs, but if conditions remain stable they well live within a six- to ten-acre covert.

In winter, the ruffed grouse's habitat may be covered with snow. If the snow is wet or dense, birds will typically roost on top of the snow or in trees. When the weather is cold and windy, and the snow deep and powdery, grouse may sleep beneath the surface for protection and warmth. Grouse movements are fairly restricted within a few acres as long as food is available in winter.

FOOD SOURCES

For the first several weeks young ruffed grouse feed entirely on insects and do not forage for the variety of foods adults consume. This high-protein animal matter is essential for chick warmth, growth, and development. Later in the summer, the poults are consuming about the same amount of animal and vegetable matter as the adults. As the season progresses the young birds eat tender shoots, green leaves, insects (if still available), all kinds of berries, and fruits. Nuts, grains, and seeds are added as they become available. When fully mature, the adults are primarily browsers, and their diet varies greatly.

The feeding patterns of ruffed grouse are like all gallinaceous birds. Feeding starts at daybreak, and continues until midmorning. Then the birds seek cooler spots with overhead cover in which to rest and dust. Later in the afternoon grouse will feed again until low light, and then go to roost at dusk.

NEIGHBORS AND HAZARDS

Early in the hunting season it is not unusual for young ruffs and blues to be in the same general area. So it is possible to confuse the two species when flushed, but once in hand their distinguishing characteristics should become evident. Most bag limits in the western states are for combinations of mountain grouse species, but still one should learn to identify each species by sight and in flight when afield. More than once I have shot both ruffs and blues in close proximity to each other. But I have never shot all three western mountain grouse species in the same general location because of their habitat differences.

Both avian and ground predators are a normal part of the ruffed grouse's life, but as with other game birds they are a small

It is not unusual for young ruffs and blues to be in the same general area.

contributor to overall mortality if the habitat provides adequate overhead shelter and concealment. Like all game birds, ruffed grouse have large clutch sizes for survival of the species. The clutch sizes of game bird species are broadly balanced to match the environment. Overall losses due to predation are fairly minimal when compared to other natural elements like weather and habitat.

READING THE COVER

The most obvious factors affecting the abundance of birds are an ample food supply and adequate year-round shelter. Together these two elements make up the birds' habitat, the foundation of their environment. The food supply also must include some form of moisture and grit. The shelter must furnish not only protection from weather and predation, but also nesting, dusting, courtship, and sunning areas. Covers that furnish adequate shelter and good food will usually produce good numbers of grouse in their explosive years.

The ruffed grouse is well known as a bird of the edges, and it seldom moves far from its core area of a dozen or so acres if ample food and shelter are available. Typical coverts are woodlands of mixed evergreens, and hardwoods with low-growing shrubs, small grassy meadows, and other openings that have multiple edges. These communities are associated with small streams, steep draws coming out of the mountain, drainages with seeps and springs, and the edges of mountain grassland parks. All of these usually have some sort of aspen community within the area or nearby, because this is the most important plant for the year-round welfare of the ruffed grouse. These complex aspen/shrub ecosystems are constantly changing, and are used quite differently by ruffed grouse during the seasons. Openings and edges of meadows that have good supplies of insects and greens are used during the summer and early fall. Brushy and overgrown areas that have a surplus of seeds, fruits, and greens are used in the fall. Mixed woodlands of

conifers and deciduous trees have fewer food supplies, but include fruits, nuts, buds, and twigs for winter and spring forage.

HUNTING TECHNIQUE

Much of the ruffed grouse habitat in the West is on state or federal lands and fairly accessible. Forest Service roads probably provide the best opportunities for locating good ruffed grouse covers.

The ruffed grouse is well known as a bird of the edges, and it seldom moves far from its core area.

As you drive along, look for pockets of grouse habitat such as side hills and draws with mixed woodlands and aspen groves. Walk old logging roads, or open skid trails that penetrate into aspen/shrub communities. Early in the hunting season ruffed grouse will often use the edges of openings along creek bottoms, meadows, and low brushy draws at lower elevations. Some of the best hunting areas for ruffed grouse are where the forest has been disturbed by human activities, or natural causes and plant succession is taking place. Small open zones that are covered with stands of quaking aspen interlocked with plum thickets, buffalo berry groves, or snowberry patches are great hangouts for grouse.

Ruffed grouse also like to forage for insects and fresh green early morning and late afternoon along old farm roads, forest openings, the edges of cut farm fields, and other sunny locations. Later in the season ruffed grouse will feed in denser cover that has openings and different edges on the forest floor.

Ruffed grouse droppings are about three-quarters to one and a quarter inches long and pencil-sized in width. One grouse can produce many droppings because much of the food it eats has little nutritional value. Ruffed grouse spend a great deal of time in openings, so droppings and dusting bowls with a few feathers in them often are easy to spot. Even a few fresh droppings are a good sign that ruffed grouse are close by. Adult ruffed grouse spend most of their lives in a small area, so work the area methodically.

Ruffed grouse are always easier to find when feeding early morning or late afternoon. Hunt along the forest edges in open parks, hayfields, pastures, berry patches, or brushy draws during feeding times. Midday, the birds are often in very dense cover, or holding up in trees, so hunt heavy hardwood covers, moist areas that have springs, aspen groves, and brushy hillsides while slowly looking up in trees for movement.

Retrievers and other flushing dogs help tremendously in finding birds in heavy cover, and the closer they work the better. Winged ruffed grouse run after getting hit, and can be very difficult to find due to their camouflage coloring. A good retriever takes the worry out of losing a fine downed ruffed grouse.

Pointing dogs also do well on ruffed grouse as most birds hold and leave a good scent. A bell or beeper collar is important in helping to locate a dog's position on point in heavy cover. My big-running dogs hold birds well, but my experience has been that western ruffed grouse often move, or fly into a tree when I arrive. I once had a pointing dog that would bark at the birds when treed. A grouse flushing out of an evergreen tree is a very challenging shot. Not only will the bird put an evergreen bough, or the trunk of the tree between you and it, but it will come off the limb in a downward arc. I can honestly say that my shooting score is much better when a bird comes off the ground than when it swoops out from a tree.

I use a super lightweight 28-gauge side-by-side with improved cylinder and modified chokes at all times when hunting ruffed grouse. A gun that is lightning quick for close shots, before the bird gets into heavy cover, is essential in the grouse woods. Any gauge shotgun is fine for ruffed grouse, but the lighter the better. When hunting any dense forest, I recommend No. 8 or 7 1/2 shot.

WESTERN RUFFED GROUSE ARE DIFFERENT

Conscientious ruffed grouse hunters always worry about whether or not they are killing too many birds out of a covert. But as something more than half of the population is lost each fall and winter anyway, it's usually safe to take two out of every five birds present during the hunting season without endangering next year's breeding stock. An eastern hunter's chance of collecting more than two birds out of a group of five in good cover typically is fairly remote, but here in the West ruffed grouse, particularly young birds, can still play the fool hen of the forest.

Although there are times when a western hunter can walk up to a family of ruffed grouse on the ground, or perched in the lower branches of an evergreen tree and possibly kill all of them, this is not what hunting is all about. And it's not good for the continuity of a healthy population of birds the following season. So I believe the old standard of two birds out of a family of five in one location is a good rule of thumb. There have been times when I could have taken a limit of young ruffs within minutes, but on every one of these occasions I have felt much better for not doing such a thing. Killing just to kill should have no part in the modern hunter's playbook. These birds do make outstanding table fare, but ethical hunting always involves some restraint.

SPRUCE GROUSE
Fool Hen

I saw my first spruce grouse one morning in the spring of 1961 while on the way to fish a high mountain lake in northern Washington. As I rounded a curve a big male spruce grouse stood quietly in a small clearing just off the trail. A single ray of sunlight had found its way through the overhead canopy of the evergreen forest, and highlighted the bird's dark tail. As I approached, he turned to face me, but didn't seem to mind my presence. I'm sure I interrupted his courtship dance. As I edged closer, he looked at me, cocked his head, flicked his tail, then flew to a low spruce limb about six feet off the ground, spreading his tail wide just before landing. He walked back and forth on the limb several times, displaying in and defending his chosen territory. After several minutes of this he returned to his original spot on the ground. I did not move, and he repeated this ritual of flying up to the limb and back to the ground.

On my way back from fishing later that afternoon, I found Mr. Grouse in the same tree, and realized how easy it would have been to miss him if I hadn't first spotted him on the ground.

ORIGINS

With the lack of fossil records, little is known of the past history of the spruce grouse. But as the spruce grouse of eastern Asia and the New World birds are so similar, it seems reasonable to assume that they share a common ancestor. After crossing the Alaskan land bridge at various times in the distant past the Siberian spruce grouse likely formed a new population that we now recognize as the North America spruce grouse.

DISTRIBUTION

Spruce grouse are dependent on short-needled conifers and gradually came to inhabit all of the coniferous forest across the northern part of North America. Their range is enormous, and of the nine grouse species of North America, only the ruffed grouse covers such an extensive geographic range. Nearly every good stand of coniferous forest in North America has its population of spruce grouse, including large portions of Canada, Alaska, and the northern reaches of the contiguous United States. The southern geographic range of the spruce grouse follows the coniferous forests across the northern part of U.S. then dips down into the Rocky Mountains of Montana, Idaho, and Wyoming and the Cascade Range in Washington and Oregon. The northern border extends to the far edges of vast treeless tundra of the Canadian provinces and Alaska.

KNOWING THE BIRD

The spruce grouse has been given many colloquial names, such as black grouse, spotted grouse, Canada grouse, wood partridge, swamp partridge, and fool hen. Of all the names, "fool hen" probably fits them best. At one time or another all of the forest grouse have been called fool hens, but today no other game bird can match this forest prince for its total lack of concern for humans, mostly due to the remoteness of where it resides.

The spruce grouse's scientific name is *Canachites canadensis*. The American Ornithologist Union recognizes four subspecies or races of spruce grouse that live in North America. The race of spruce grouse living in the Rocky Mountain region is designated as the Franklin's spruce grouse (*C. c. franklinii*). The neighboring race to the north is the Hudsonian spruce grouse (*C. c. canadensis*), covering most of the Canadian interior. This book deals mainly with these two subspecies. All of the races are very similar in appearance, but upon close examination there are some subtle plumage differences in different regions of the bird's range. For the purposes of this book, the individual subspecies will simply be lumped together under the name spruce grouse.

A spruce grouse is a medium-sized mountain game bird averaging fifteen to seventeen inches long, with a wingspan of twenty-three to twenty-four inches, and a weight of one and a quarter to one and a half pounds. The sexes are quite different in coloration. The male is barred, with black and gray on the back

The sexes are quite different in coloration. Females are more mottled and lighter in color than the male.

and white and black on the lower belly. The breast and throat are black, bordered with white and with a red comb. Females have more mottled colors of black and brown on the back; copper and black on the throat and upper breast; and brown, black, and white on the belly. Both male and female have leg feathers to the toes. The Franklin's grouse has a distinctive rust band on the tail, which is lacking on the other three races of spruce grouse.

Spruce grouse make a loud whirring sound when flushed from the ground or a tree. The birds fly to the heaviest cover available, twisting and turning through the timber. In flight, both sexes appear dark in color with a wide black tail that is shorter than the tail of other forest grouse.

LIFE CYCLE

In the northwestern states, breeding starts in late April, and lasts through the end of May. The hen nests in June, and the brood is hatched around the first week of July. Nests are usually well concealed under a low branch, and are often located in an evergreen thicket. She lays four to ten eggs, the average being six. Incubation takes about twenty-one days. Upon leaving the nest the young brood fans out ahead of the female to feed. Chicks depend on insects in the first several weeks to develop quickly. The mother does not lead them to food, but occasionally will fly ahead to call them to a better feeding area. The female grouse is an extremely good mother, and can be highly aggressive toward intruders approaching her brood. Her first move is to try to decoy the danger away, but if this fails she will come to the aid of her chicks.

Young birds develop rapidly, and within a week can fly to a low branch. Within three weeks, juveniles can fly as well as the hen to get to a high tree limb or a thicket to avoid danger. Spruce grouse do not flock up, but families do join together in groups of up to a dozen chicks. Young grouse mortality can vary depending on the quality of cover, but the rate is similar to other mountain grouse species with the same long-term population cycles. There is very little information about the longevity of individual spruce grouse, but three to five years would be a very long life. In late summer the birds stay in loose family groups, often in singles or pairs. But like their forest cousins, spruce grouse do experience a fall break up, or fall shuffle, in which family groups disperse over a wide area.

FOOD SOURCES

The spruce grouse does not migrate, but is subject to seasonal shifts prompted more by food issues than weather. During late spring, summer, and early fall food sources vary, although they typically consume large quantities of conifer needles. The birds relish insects, bursting buds, green leaves, berries, and forbs as soon as they become available. As long as ground food is available spruce grouse will take advantage of it. From late fall to early spring the largest part of the bird's diet is made up of conifer needles. The kind of needles eaten depends on the area in which the birds live. These various conifers include larch, pines, fir, and spruce. At this time of year most feeding takes place in trees. In cold weather, or if snow covers the ground, grouse seek out even denser evergreen cover, and rarely move from place to place for days at a time.

Spruce grouse start feeding at first light, and continue for several hours. They feed again from late afternoon until dusk, and then roost in trees. Midday is reserved for gritting, dusting, and lofting on the forest floor in any available openings, such as at the base of a large tree. The spruce grouse also utilizes natural and man-made openings to collect grit and perform other daily functions. Resting during the day takes place ten to fifteen feet above the forest floor on an open limb in an evergreen tree.

NEIGHBORS AND HAZARDS

It is relatively unusual to find spruce grouse and ruffed grouse hanging out in the same general locations because of differing habitat demands, but it can happen during a part of the fall season. Ruffed grouse are much more stationary, remaining in a small area, but spruce grouse will occasionally move into the same living space for a short time. If the habitat meets their needs for food and cover it is quite possible for more than one forest grouse

It is relatively unusual to find spruce grouse and ruffed grouse hanging out in the same general locations because of differing habitat demands, but it can happen during a part of the fall season.

to be in the same location, at least briefly. But it is fairly unlikely for the hunter to find all three mountain grouse species together because they tend to concentrate at different elevations as the season progresses.

Avian and ground predators share the spruce grouse's range, but as with other birds, predation only plays a small role in overall mortality as long as good cover is present to provide shelter from bad weather and concealment. Population stability over time is a function of abundant food and good cover, long-term climate trends, local weather, predation, and other hazards.

READING THE COVER

In the West the strongest spruce grouse population occurs west of the Continental Divide, beyond the Rocky Mountain Front. Still, eastern slopes of the Rockies that blend into foothill plains and some isolated mountain ranges hold good numbers of spruce grouse. Here the birds favor both lower and higher elevations of heavy mature forests that are closely associated with spruce/fir, and other mixed coniferous forests.

The forests that spruce grouse prefer fall into three categories: dense, denser, and downright impenetrable. Much of this forest cover supports lodgepole pine, Engelmann spruce, fir, and some western larch, with a foot or so of understory composed of low-growing

The forest that spruce grouse prefer fall into three categories: dense, denser, and downright impenetrable.

shrubs. This cover can make for hard walking. Spruce grouse use small, open, grassy zones with stands of buffalo berry, huckleberry, and snowberry seasonally.

The birds also like to use southern slopes with good sun exposure more than other locations. Later in the season spruce grouse use denser cover types. This type of heavy conifer forest is most common between elevations of three thousand to six thousand feet. It requires some knowledge to understand the subtle differences in flora within spruce grouse territory, but it's well worth the time to learn.

HUNTING TECHNIQUE

Much of the best spruce grouse hunting occurs on state and federal lands, accessible via Forest Service access roads. Once in spruce grouse country, walk old logging roads, open skid trails, and other openings that penetrate the dense forest. Good hunting can often be found where dense forest gives way to power

The forest that spruce grouse prefer fall into three categories: dense, denser, and downright impenetrable.

line clearings, burned-over sites, logging operations, and roads and trails. Early in the hunting season spruce grouse will often use openings along creek bottoms and low brushy draws at higher elevation, although not as much at lower elevations.

The coniferous forest in which the birds live is sometimes difficult to penetrate. I believe the most important factor for hunting spruce grouse is finding the right habitat type in relationship to the right elevation. Walking trails, working open southern slopes, walking the edges of dense woods, and seeking open berry patches and moist areas with heavy cover will net the best results.

Spruce grouse droppings come in different shades of greens, and are quite similar to domestic chicken excretions. But as the birds spend a great deal of time in heavy cover and in trees, locating droppings can be difficult. Search open clearings in the forest floor for any bird sign, such as droppings or dusting bowls with feathers. Even a few fresh droppings will indicate that grouse are close by, so work the area methodically.

The spruce grouse has short cupped wings, typical of all forest grouse. The wings are designed for quick takeoffs and acrobatic flight, but are not suited for long-distance flying. Flight speeds are fairly slow, and the birds usually fly only a short distance from ground to tree. They often refuse to fly at all when approached by a hunter, but a true sportsperson will only shoot the bird on the wing. When the bird does fly, it can present a difficult target as it weaves between trees to put obstacles between itself and the gunner. Although spruce grouse really do deserve the moniker fool hen, they can still fool the hunter at times.

Having a dog along can save many hours of valuable time in search of birds. Even when they are flushed out of range, it's usually easy to mark their location because they fly short distances. I like to work more than one dog at a time to cover a lot of ground. Spruce grouse spend many hours in trees, out of sight of ground dwellers, so walk slowly. Along the borders of openings and brushy creeks a dog is especially helpful in finding a bird that a hunter would pass by. Bells or electronic location collars are helpful for keeping track of dogs in heavy cover. When a grouse is flushed from the ground it invariably goes to dense cover, typically an evergreen tree. Getting the grouse out of the tree can be a real challenge, and it presents a very difficult wing shot. If the hunter is lucky enough to get a shot and put a bird on the ground a dog is invaluable to finding the grouse in such dense cover.

Close-working dogs of any sporting breed are very beneficial when hunting forest grouse. And dogs that retrieve or track wounded birds are downright essential. All grouse will run, even when wounded. They like to go to the heaviest cover when pursued, the kind only a dog can negotiate.

I once hunted with a guy who used a springer spaniel. I was working two big-running pointers across the creek from him. Both of us were hunting steep brushy mixed forest slopes, which made walking difficult. One of my dogs went on point in a small opening, but the five young spruce grouse flushed before I had a chance to get into gun range. The birds scattered, crossing the creek and landing in a thicket on a steep slope high above my hunting partner. Calling my dogs in, I stayed on my side of the creek and watched the episode unfold. His close-working springer hit the dense cover with tail wagging and flushed each bird one by one. My fiend's game bag had more lumps in it than mine.

I use a super lightweight 28-gauge side-by-side with improved cylinder and modified chokes most of the time. On occasion, I use my lovable old classic Ithaca Model 37, 16-gauge featherweight pump for spruce grouse too. I like these two shotguns because they are lightning quick at close range. Any gauge shotgun is fine for mountain grouse, but the lighter the better. When hunting any dense forest the shot size I recommend is No. 8 or 7 1/2.

BIRDS OF THE DENSE FOREST

One of my most memorable encounters with spruce grouse came one bright sunny day while I was walking a trail in an isolated mountain range. By ten o'clock in the morning the carpet of brilliant red and gold leaves glistened in the sun filtering through the thick canopy of spruce trees. Dewdrops clung to the leafless bushes brushing against my pant legs, and the moist forest floor cushioned every step. Good places for big dark grouse to feed, fattening up before winter, I thought.

Following the hiking trail toward a distant mountain lake at five thousand feet, I decided that mid-morning would be the best time for the spruce grouse to be feeding in the openings on the forest floor, before it heated up and put the birds in the trees. Sometimes the trail grew steep, other times it flattened out, and put small sweet-smelling puddles of water in my path. I moved slowly to listen for any birds that might flush close by.

For the first hour my young prairie-hunting partner Winston seemed unsure of himself. He would run far up the trail, then return to me for encouragement, not sure of what to do with the deep woods. Eventually, he gained more confidence and started making short loops in the woods, coming out on the trail behind me. As the loops lengthened, the sound of his bell would fade, and I would stand still and strain to hear it stop. It wasn't too long

A good day of spruce grouse hunting is not measured by the number of birds in the bag, but by the number of points.

before Winton got the hang of things and started locking down on birds. Once his bell stopped sounding I'd enter the woods, shotgun ready, looking for a white spot in a dark background. After several points and flushes I still hadn't cut a single feather. I hoped young Winston wasn't keeping score.

Toward early afternoon, when the woods slowly began to dim, I started the return trip to the pickup. Winston had been hunting hard all day, and began to shorten his woodland casts considerably. By the time he made his last point the forest had become so dark that I couldn't distinguish any light color at all. Silence accompanied each methodical step I took on the soft forest duff. The bird flushed under my feet just as I eased around a large spruce tree. Winston was looking straight into my eyes from twenty feet away. Instantly I shot high above his head, and the bird dropped at his feet. He put the big male grouse in my hand, looking up at me as if to say, "Sometimes we have to trap the bird to get a good shot."

Back at the truck, I laid the bird on the floor of the back seat and drove down the steep logging road. Winston had curled up on the front seat and was already asleep. I put my hand on his head, and as he sighed I thanked him for the number of grouse he found and murmured, "A good day of spruce grouse hunting is not measured by the number of birds in the bag, but by the number of points."

BLUE GROUSE
Mountain Blues

I was hunting along a line of quaking aspens on the edge
of an open meadow in the mountains of western Montana
when I shot my first blue grouse. My Brittany, Gina, had
frozen along an old logging road that wound along a mountain
drainage. There was a commotion off the trail, then a burst of
wings, as three blue grouse rocketed up out of a large patch of
snowberries and headed into the quakies. One blue landed in an
opening on the ground nearby, while the other two flew beyond
the aspen grove. The lone bird picked the ground and flicked
its tail, watching the motionless dog, which was trembling
like an aspen leaf. After a few tense moments she flushed. The
20-gauge over-under barked, and the echo ricocheted off the

steep canyon walls as nothing, but a few aspen leaves drifted to the ground.

The forest grew silent again as I walked empty-handed through the aspen grove toward the other birds. As I approached, one of the blue grouse came into view on a bare limb halfway up a forty-foot fir tree. It stretched out its neck and looked at me with great curiosity. After I threw several large sticks, and with the dog causing quite a fuss beneath the tree, the grouse became nervous and flushed. Shooting a bird swooping down out of a tree is not easy, but I got lucky and centered the grouse at twenty yards, just before it would have swerved out of sight. Gina immediately ran toward the large gray-blue hen, sniffed it, then picked it up and brought my first blue grouse to hand.

ORIGINS

The blue grouse seems to have originated in the mountainous conifer forest–grasslands region of western North America during the late Pleistocene. It is interesting to note that this bird shares physical and behavioral traits with both forest and prairie grouse. There is evidence to suggest that blue grouse may have evolved from the prairie sage grouse's ancestor since both species utilize shrub/steppe high-desert habitat during much of the year. But in winter blue grouse move to higher mountain elevations where other forest grouse live.

DISTRIBUTION

The range of the blue grouse covers most of Alaska, and extends south along the mountains of western Canada and the U.S., reaching as far down as Mexico. This vast area includes virtually all of the mountains ranges in western North America, including the isolated outlying ranges.

KNOWING THE BIRD

Blue grouse have been called other names such as dusky grouse, sooty grouse, gray grouse, and pine grouse, and over the years they have sometimes been classified as different species or as a single species. These days the consensus among taxonomists seems to be that there are two species: the dusky grouse (*Dendragapus obscurus*), which occupies the Rocky Mountains, and the sooty grouse (*Dendragapus fuliginosus*), which typically inhabits the Pacific Coast Ranges and the Sierra Nevada. These two groups occur over a wide range of habitats from sea-level rainforest and shrub/steppe high desert to subalpine and high-elevation alpine tundra. They all usually migrate to similar high, dense conifer forests in winter where needles become their main food.

Blue grouse are the largest of the mountain grouse, and the second largest game bird in the North American family Tetraonidae, which includes all of the grouse, ptarmigan, and prairie chickens. The male blue grouse is twenty to twenty-two inches long, has a wingspan of about twenty-eight inches, and weighs up to four pounds. The female is seventeen to eighteen inches long, and weighs about three pounds.

The male has mostly grayish or slate-colored plumage with a yellow orange comb above the eyes, and a slightly crested head. The female is somewhat smaller and different in coloration, with a more mottled brown overall. Both sexes have a long, squared

Blue grouse are the largest of the mountain grouse.

tail with a gray band at the end, although some birds in the interior Rockies lack the band.

Blue grouse are not very vocal when alarmed, and prefer to run on the ground instead of flying if at all possible. When flushed, blues have a loud, rapid takeoff, and quickly put a tree between themselves and the intruder. When flushed on a ridge they will drop down over the side to gain speed as quickly a possible. On hillsides, they prefer to fly around the hill, going slightly downhill until out of sight. Blues have fast wing motions, and can twist and turn around branches and trees. In flight the adult male appears very dark in color with a wide tail. The female and juveniles appear similar in flight but smaller.

LIFE CYCLE

As winter ends in the mountains, and as soon as the snow cover permits, the male blue arrives on its summer range, and establishes a territorial breeding ground. The males become extremely territorial at this time, and will restrict all of their daily movements and activities to this area. These territorial sites are at lower elevations than the wintering grounds, and vary within subspecies because of different habitat localities. Display sites may include an open raised forest floor, fallen logs, rocks, and open tree limbs. Males hoot to attract a female. In some locations they use high evergreen trees to hoot, and in other places they'll call from a log or the ground. Breeding takes place on the territorial range from around late March to mid-May, depending on the elevation and region. After breeding, males become fairly solitary, and may start to move to higher timbered areas.

Females occupy the nest site alone, and are never within a male's breeding territory. Nesting and brood raising occur at much lower elevations than the male breeding area or the birds' winter range. Nests are always on the ground, and usually have some sort of overhead canopy. A nest may be up against a large dead log, stump, or live tree. The hen blue grouse makes a shallow bowl-shaped nest in soft soil, and lines it sparsely with dead leaves, needles, a few feathers, and other debris within reach.

The hen's clutch consists of seven to ten eggs, and incubation takes about twenty-three days. After hatching, the female and her brood stay together as a family group during the summer. Blue grouse chicks are fairly independent, and can fly short distances in six or seven days.

The young chicks feed almost entirely on insects during their first month, and will consume animal matter as long as available. During the summer months blue grouse families are often associated with mixed grass-forbs cover around the edges of open meadows in the foothills of the mountains. Later the birds will use more bushy hardwood thickets, and begin to abandon their summer brood range. In early autumn, depending on weather and the abundance of food, the female will move the juveniles to higher open areas, and some mixing with other families may occur. At about this same time the females will start to leave their brood behind, and move to the birds' traditional wintering grounds at higher elevations. As the season progresses the juveniles will also begin to move, singly, or in small groups, to higher slopes on the way to their wintering areas in the coniferous zones.

As with all upland game birds, the morality rate of blues is high. Studies indicate 50 to 65 percent of young grouse don't make it through to fall, and one third of the adults die annually. The blue grouse life span is a bit longer than most upland game birds, and research has shown that a few birds may live to an old age of ten or twelve years.

FOOD SOURCES

Although the various blue grouse subspecies occupy a wide range of habitat types, their food requirements are much the same, and consist mostly of vegetation. Only in summer and early fall do the adults and young feed on animal matter gleaned from the edges of open parks and alpine meadows. During this period of insect feeding they can be a long way from any thick overhead cover. Once the insects dwindle the juveniles turn to brushier habitat to feed on berries, fruits, leaves, seeds, flowers, and many other herbaceous plants. From spring to late fall, blues

During the period of insect feeding blues can be a long way from any thick overhead cover.

do not migrate, but make a seasonal shift toward higher elevations in search of different food types. Once on their wintering grounds within high conifer forests the birds focus entirely on the needles of Douglas fir, ponderosa pine, and hemlocks. In late fall and winter blue grouse feed early in the morning, rest and loaf midday, and then feed intensively again in the last three hours of light.

NEIGHBORS AND HAZARDS

If the habitat meets the food and cover needs of more than one forest grouse species it is quite possible to find them in the same general area. But it remains unlikely that all three species of mountain grouse would be in close proximity to one another at any given time. It's not unusual to find ruffed grouse and spruce grouse or ruffed grouse and blue grouse hanging out in the same general locations early in the hunting season, although it's rare for spruce and blue grouse to congregate in the same mountainous elevation areas. That fact is, I often plan to hunt blue and ruffed grouse in the same area early in the year.

Ground and avian predators are present throughout much of the blue grouse's range, but losses to predators are fairly minimal as long as good cover is present. Like all game birds, blue grouse bring off a large family brood to maintain a breeding population for the following season.

READING THE COVER

Blue grouse will be found on their summer range early in the hunting season. Many times they are found in the same habitat and location as ruffed grouse. In fall, the grouse family will occupy terrain with open meadows on lower mountain slopes, along foothills, and in isolated parks below the dense conifer forests. Look for mixed hardwood/evergreen draws with creeks running through them, sagebrush side hills, brush patches with berries and fruit, aspen groves, and grassy pastures. As changing weather brings frost and cold nights to their summer range, the birds move to higher elevations with the arrival of winter. Blue grouse winter habitat is mixed conifer forest (with Douglas fir), and the best zones are the open parks (small grassy areas) on wide ridges.

HUNTING TECHNIQUE

Hunting blues early in the season requires different tactics than hunting them later. Early on, young blue grouse are still locked into their summer brood range far from the shadows of the high mountain ridges where the birds winter. In summer and early fall blue grouse occupy many of the same areas as ruffed grouse, but not necessarily the same intermountain shrub grassland habitat. The difference is that blues utilize more open lands, such as sagebrush areas, hillsides with fruit-laden berries patches, sparse brushy hardwood draws, open unused roads, cutover areas, and summer pastures. Ruffed grouse are more associated with smaller opening close to thick understory with high canopy cover. Ruffs seldom venture far into open spaces, and use only the open edges next to tight cover to forge for food. Look for blue grouse in berry patches and grassy meadows early in the morning or in late afternoon. Work creek bottoms and moist draws with mixed forest types around midday.

My real passion for hunting blue grouse comes late in the season when the young birds move to higher winter zones. Even though climbing to the ridge tops becomes much harder, I walk slowly, enjoy the autumn scenery, and know the birds are well worth the effort. Much of the blue grouse's winter range lies within our national forests, so access is plentiful. Follow forest roads into the mountains, and head up to ridges and open parks where blue grouse winter. Finding winter grounds can be difficult at times, but the payoff is large as the birds tend to be more concentrated than when on their summer range. Look for mountain ridges that are fairly flat and wide with mixed coniferous forest, open meadows (parks), and rocky outcroppings. Many times the birds will be along the edges of the ridge, and not far from rock outcroppings with steep slopes.

Keep a lookout for evidence that birds are present. Blue grouse leave a lot of droppings that are chicken-like in size and light to dark green in color. Good areas to look for droppings include loggings roads,

Early in the hunting season blue grouse are still locked into their summer brood range far from the shadows of the high mountain ridges where the birds winter.

trails, and clearings in the forest and under possible roosting trees. Dusting bowls are another clear sign that birds are close by. Look for these little scooped-out places in soft soil, possibly with a few feathers in them, in small open areas on the forest floor.

Blue grouse spend many hours feeding and resting in trees, so hunting the same location at different times of day can be rewarding. When flushed out of a tree the birds dive to gain speed, which makes shooting a challenge. These fast fliers will often pitch off a ridge with strong wing beats, set their wings, and glide down the mountain.

Any breed of bird dog can be beneficial when hunting blue grouse. Many birds are shot flying into heavy cover and they can be difficult to locate on the ground. Blue grouse are strong runners after being winged and birds that dive over a hill or ridge after

Any breed of dog can be beneficial when hunting blue grouse.

being shot are impossible to mark down. These birds are easily lost without the help of a dog that hunts dead and retrieves. Flushing and retrieving breeds are a big help in pushing blues from brushy cover. Pointing dogs are useful in open meadows and on brushy slopes where large areas need to be covered. Many times, blue grouse will flush into a tree, and be out of sight before the hunter arrives, yet lingering scent on the ground still may help a dog determine if birds are present.

I use a super lightweight 28-gauge side-by-side with improved cylinder and modified chokes most of the time when chasing mountain grouse. On occasion, I still use my lovable old classic Ithaca Model 37, 16-gauge featherweight pump. But any gauge shotgun is fine as long as you remember that lightness makes for easier walking in rugged country. And most shots at blue grouse come at close range, so the faster the gun the quicker the shot. When hunting any dense forest I recommend No. 7 1/2 shot, which will penetrate heavy cover well enough.

LATE MOUNTAIN BLUES

Hunting blue grouse late in the season requires a different playbook. The situation is so unlike hunting the early season that it is safe to say it's almost like hunting a different game bird. Blues winter in high rugged country and logging roads and wilderness trails always seem to lead uphill. Walking is always rough, so good lug-soled boots and a

Much of the blue grouse's winter range lies within our national forests, so access is plentiful

strong-running dog are required. The type of cover also requires a dog to be controlled, and a staunch point helps hold birds until you arrive.

Blues are the mavericks of the mountain grouse. They're movers—here today, gone tomorrow. An occasional blue grouse shares the skillet with scrambled eggs and fried potatoes at big game hunting camp, but for the most part these hunters would rather not let those shots ring out in the woods for fear of scaring their main quarry. I have never crossed paths with a rifle hunter in the woods during the late season, although in some places I'm sure it's possible. But unlike early-rising big game hunters, bird hunters typically arrive in the woods long after the forest has awakened. The optimum time of day to hunt is when the birds are actively feeding, which means my hunting schedule starts about ten-thirty, and ends around three-thirty. So by the time I get in the woods most respectable deer and elk hunters are home, or in camp taking a nap. But be aware that others may be in the woods, so wear a blaze orange hat and vest.

The advantage of hunting late-season mountain grouse is that the birds are fully grown. Scenting conditions are much better too, because adult birds give off a lot more scent, and the smell of green vegetation is gone. The hardwoods and shrubs are void of leaves, opening up the understory beneath the canopy of trees and making it easier to see. Also, the dogs are able to work harder and cover more ground during cool or cold weather.

The biggest disadvantage of hunting blue grouse late season is what happens on the ground. My rule of thumb is that a skiff to three inches of snow is ideal, but after that I don't recommend hunting. Dry powdery snow and cold weather seem to suit my dogs best, and they can run for hours. They seem to sense where the birds are long before I do, but I do not just walk aimlessly along a logging road or trail. I make a plan based on logic, starting with how much snow is on the ground, and the type of terrain to be hunted. Knowing the birds' winter habits and habitat is extremely useful, and probably more important than it is at other times of the year. For instance, we may hunt from aspen grove to aspen grove for ruffed grouse, or head to patches of snowberry in high open meadows for blues.

Listen for ground movements and sounds while you walk. A single grouse flushing can help you locate other birds. Follow the sound, for it will reveal to you where the birds are feeding or resting and the type of cover they are using. Some days, this is the key that opens the door to other likely covers where birds are feeding.

Once the snow becomes too deep for the dogs to work effectively my mountain grouse season ends. For me, without dogs there is no hunt.

BEFORE AND AFTER THE GAME

The Hunting Wagon

What are the prerequisites for a prairie wagon? It has to be rugged, reliable, have high clearance, and be able to hold a hunter or two, a couple of dogs, and a lot of gear. My first hunting rig, a blue VW Bug, did all that and more.

My first trip in the Bug was a blue grouse hunt in the Cascade Mountains of Washington. Over coffee, eggs, and bacon, a logging friend of mine had drawn a map on a napkin showing the route to my intended destination.

"It's a rough, muddy road. If you don't make it back, I'll be up there Monday morning," he said.

The penciled drawing was lying on my thigh as I followed the line with my finger, one eye on the map, and the other on the rough logging road. The best blue grouse hunting is always on the highest ridge. On the map, the last mile was circled and scribbled "steep," and the logger said I might have to walk that since I didn't have a four-wheel drive. In those days, the only four-by-four vehicles available were surplus military jeeps, a few big cumbersome Travelalls, and pickup trucks that cost three times as much as a Volkswagen Bug. I figured I could walk if need be. The last hill was steep, but there were also fresh tire tracks. I put the car in low, revved up the little air-cooled engine, and started up the steep incline. When I got to the top, I parked next to an old, olive-green jeep without a canvas top.

My two Brittanys, Gina and Lola, and I hunted a couple of hours, and returned to the VW for water and lunch, where I found a note lying on the hood next to the windshield wiper:

We saw you coming up the hill, and I made a bet with my hunting buddy that you couldn't make it. Hope you have good grouse hunting. We did.

P.S. Never saw one of those German cars before. I lost the bet—have a drink on me.

There was an Oly beer holding down the note.

By the time the little blue's odometer turned over and started at zero again, I was hunting pronghorn antelope in the backcountry, and the blue Beetle was well known across much of the sagebrush prairies of eastern Montana.

It seemed like an hour before I got back to gravel on the country road. At the check station, a game warden was checking a nice buck antelope. I pulled in back of a parked Chevy pickup and stopped. When the pickup left, the officer walked over as I was getting out of the VW.

"Been hunting?" he asked. "No luck yet?"

"Yes, sir," I answered smiling. "I shot a young buck pronghorn."

He looked at me, then at my muddy blue Bug and said, "Did you leave it in the backcountry?"

"No, sir." I reached through the window of the VW and released the hood lock. "It's in the front trunk. The trunk popped open halfway from the pressure.

He raised the hood and looked in amazement at the antelope. He checked my license and the filled-out tag on the buck. "You could have fooled me," he exclaimed.

Whatever vehicle you drive, always use common sense and be prepared for hazardous conditions. Never take a chance in the backcountry. I've had to walk out twice—fifteen miles once due to snow and ten another time after losing my keys—but not anymore. I always check snow depth before plowing through it, and I learned to tape a key to the underside of my vehicle.

Early season hunting is usually the easiest time to get around, but there are some rules that should always be observed. The safest bet is to stay on roads or trails used by the rancher on private land—they appreciate it—and designated roads on public land. By staying on a road, all kinds of hazards can be avoided. Driving across open prairie, you may not be able to see deep holes, rocks, barbed wire, or low, wet areas. Never cross a moist area unless it has been previously traveled, and even then I walk through it to make sure the ground is solid. I never cross a watercourse unless one set of my vehicles, wheels rests on dry ground. I do not believe in road hunting for game birds, so once I leave the vehicle to hunt, I return only for fresh dogs, water, and maybe lunch.

A shovel, axe, jack, spare tire, towline, chains, four-way lug wrench, and extra keys should be standard equipment that is never left at home. Other useful equipment if four-wheeling in rugged terrain, or in isolated places is a high-lift bumper jack, and a come-along or winch. Having a cellular phone in your hunting rig can be very useful, and they work well in most areas today.

Whatever kind of vehicle you drive, make sure you know its capability. From my VW Bug days to the present I've had many hunting rigs. All but the little blue Bug have been four-by-four pickups, small and large. These days, a four-door Toyota Tundra fits my requirements for hunting at home and across America. But no matter what the vehicle, make sure it's equipped for the kind of upland hunting you do, with or without dogs.

What do I carry in my K-9 Hilton pickup? First, it has a white fiberglass, dog-equipped topper containing six compartments for twelve dogs. Each compartment is well ventilated, waterproof, and has a waste drain. I like the white topper because it stays cool in direct sunlight. I have never had a dog get overheated—or cold—in these compartments. If the weather is extremely hot, only one dog goes in each space when the vehicle is stationary.

Below the dog compartments, in the bed of the pickup, are two large sliding drawers. When pulled out, they are supported by the tailgate. Each six-foot drawer has ample room for hunting gear, dog gear and food, warm- and cold-weather clothing, and other items such as an icebox, toolbox, small water jugs, and a first-aid kit. In the center is a removable ladder for the dogs and a six-foot-long container made from PVC pipe that holds thirteen gallons of water.

With a full-sized cab, there's plenty of room for two people, twelve dogs, and all the equipment needed for a long trip. And for a trip of less than a hundred miles, there is ample room for four hunters and gear.

Aside from basic equipment that should always be in the hunting rig, I break other accessories into two categories: dog safety and comfort, and the hunter's needs.

Occasionally, I have forgotten small items, and most of them are for the dogs. Now, I have accumulated all the dog essentials in several large containers, and never take them out of my pickup. I make a note of any item missing or depleted, and replace it at once. Dog essentials that I have in my hunting rig at all times include:

- Container of water, large and small
- Large watering pans
- Water bottles
- Combs
- Rope
- Leads
- Blanket
- Half a dozen dog whistles
- Extra pins for dog compartment doors
- Recall collars
- Body protectors
- Dog boots
- Duct tape
- Forceps of different sizes
- First-aid kit for humans and dogs

I believe my first-aid kit had everything except an operating table. My veterinarian supplies me with items necessary for any minor accident in the field, ranging from antibiotics to a staple gun. I don't use a standard first-aid box because it's too small. Instead, I have an eleven-by-eleven-by-nineteen-inch plastic toolbox. This box never leaves the hunting rig.

Bird hunters have to dress for walking conditions. When walking, you have to consider the long-range weather forecast, and the time of day you will be in the field. Other considerations are the type of vegetation, terrain, and birds you are hunting. I start out dressed in fairly light clothing, because there is nothing worse than being sweaty all day.

I'm not going to discuss every article of gear. For one thing, most hunters already have a comfortable uniform. And for another, new synthetic clothing is advancing so rapidly that it's too difficult

Occasionally, I have forgotten small items, but not anymore. Now, I have accumulated all the dog essentials in several large containers.

to keep up with all the new hunting attire anyway. I do, however, keep enough extra clothing in my truck to outfit a football team, including hats, vest, socks, shirts, pants, undergarments, and gloves—all in various sizes. It's about as difficult to tell guests what to wear hunting as it is to convince someone to change political parties.

Nevertheless, let's have a look at a couple of things I think are important. I learned from long experience that armies, football teams, and hunters all move on their stomachs and feet. I won't get into the stomach part, but boots—good boots—are the most important item on my list. There is no such thing as one perfect boot made for all upland bird hunting. I recommend a high, full-leather, lace-up boot with good ankle support and a rubber lug sole. Later in the season, I prefer a high, leather, lace-up, insulated, Gortex waterproof boot because of snow and cold weather. I don't use lightweight boots because they sacrifice ruggedness and good ankle support.

Next on my list are pants. I like them tough enough to go through stickers and briars, but light enough for good movement. I prefer a vest to a coat, even when it's cold. With today's clothing, keeping warm is not a problem, and I like to keep my arms free of too many layers.

Hats, shirts, socks, underwear, gloves, and other garments are personal as far as I'm concerned, and there are all kinds of choices out there. For the last couple of years I have been wearing gaiters called Turtleskin SnakeArmor, made by Warwick Mills. They are extremely lightweight, easy to put on, fit well, and are wonderful protection, not only for poisonous snakes, but also for walking in grasslands and brush country.

HAZARDS OF THE GAME

Because there are many pleasures associated with hunting, it's easy to forget about the hazards that man or dog may meet. These are unpredictable and can ruin a day's hunt—even a whole trip. Most accidents can be treated in the field, a few cannot. My advice to every dog owner going into the field to hunt is to obtain a first-aid book, such as The Orvis Field Guide to First Aid for Sporting Dogs, by Charles DeVinne, DVM.

Probably the most feared hazard is the poisonous snake. Before going afield in snake country, contact your veterinarian about snake-bite prevention, and what to do if your dog does get bitten.

Over the years, I have walked hundreds of miles in snake country with a herd of dogs. I may have been lucky, but in the fifty-plus years I've worked dogs in the field I've had only eighteen dogs bitten, none fatally. One dog was bitten on two different occasions. After the second time, he got scared when I moved the garden hose, or when he saw a stick.

Sometimes dogs will point a rattlesnake, but not always. It seems to me that they associate it with something to be hunted, which is why I never shoot a snake in my dogs' presence. Most of my adult dogs steer clear of any snake, ever after pointing the critters.

Rattlesnakes are widely distributed throughout most of North America. My experience is only with western prairie rattlesnakes. The western rattler is a lot less dangerous than most of the other twenty-nine species. My viewpoint may be a little different than other folks. I have had little trouble with rattlesnakes over the years, and prefer not to kill them. I see ten to twenty rattlers annually while training and hunting, but I simply call the dogs away, and go around them.

Beyond considerations of training, I believe rattlesnakes have their place in the natural world, and are beneficial in killing rodents that harm nesting game birds. While it is true that snakes eat bird eggs too, the amount is trivial when compared to the number of rodents they consume. Besides that, I think rattlers are pretty decent, usually (but not always) giving a hunter and his

Rattlesnakes may be present in many places on the high plains, so the best prevention is to understand their behavior, and make decisions accordingly.

dogs plenty of warning. Once you hear that buzz, you'll never forget the sound.

Other than actually seeing a poisonous snake bite your dog, how do you know if your dog has been bitten? The dog quits hunting, slows down, walks behind you for a short time, then curls up, and tries to go to sleep. After a while, other obvious signs appear. The dog will start to salivate, hang its head, and sometimes vomit, but the best clue is swelling around the bite area.

When a dog is bitten, the first thing I do is calm the dog, and go back to the hunting rig as quickly as possible. Every one of my dogs that has been bitten has been a long way from any vet at the time. But still my advice is to take the dog to a veterinarian as soon as possible. One of the worst areas for a dog to get bitten is on the nose. The head quickly swells up, and the dog is not recognizable. It salivates or drools constantly.

A couple of years ago one of my older females got hit while in a patch of high snowberries. I didn't see the snake, but heard her yelp, and went to investigate. The other three dogs were pointing beyond the brush patch, and I figured a stick poked her while she was moving up to back them. I checked her over and she appeared fine after the Huns flushed. We were a stone's throw from the hunting rig, and I put her in the dog compartment, unaware of her condition. I did not realize that she was hurt until the next morning when she couldn't get up. My veterinarian and I looked her over very closely and couldn't find any evidence of snakebite, but her symptoms indicated otherwise. After medication and rest, she recovered in a few days.

Rattlesnakes may be present during much of the hunting season. I have encountered them as late as the end of October, but as the season progresses, chances for finding an active snake diminish. However, I don't let their presence alter my plans. If you are concerned, I suggest you avoid rock piles, rocky slopes, and rock outcroppings on warm days. Even so, there are no guarantees for dogs, because they run all over; my dogs may cover twenty times more country than I do, and I'm sure they encounter a lot more snakes that I care to think about. Just remember that snakes do not lie in wait for dogs, or chase them. The best prevention is to understand the behavior of snakes, and make decisions accordingly.

I consider porcupines more of a threat to a dog than western rattlesnakes. Why? Because I have had more disastrous encounters with them. Whether it is the smell, the lure of a large, slow-moving object, or just curiosity, I don't know, but dogs seem to be attracted to porcupines, and I find it much harder to break them of their curiosity for those prickly critters than I do snakes.

Unlike with a rattlesnake bite, I don't leave the field when a porcupine strikes. Instead, I extract the quills as quickly as possible. On one occasion a single porcupine hit four of my dogs. Luckily my wife was along, and after almost an hour we had removed over a hundred quills. This is why good, high-quality forceps are a necessity. They should be long and have a strong bite. I carry one on my whistle lanyard, one in my hunting vest, and one more in the dog supply box in the hunting rig. If another person is along I have them carry a pair too. Never go without them, but if you do forget you can always use your teeth to pull most of the quills out before going back to the hunting rig.

You will often hear that cutting the end of the quills can make them easier to remove. Don't believe it. It takes too much time, and you need as much quill length as possible for pulling. Pull the most lethal quills first—down the throat, under the tongue, and around the neck. Legs and feet are not vital areas, so pull those quills last.

People always ask me how you control the dog when pulling quills. Most dogs settle down after several quills are removed, but don't start pulling the ones from the lips or tongue first because these are very sensitive areas. If the dog does not cooperate, there are several things I try to do. I put the dog on its back, and tie all four legs together, or have someone hold them. I also throw a coat over the dog. If I'm back at the vehicle, I use a blanket to wrap the dog up. If there are quills in the mouth—and there usually are—I put my belt or lead, if available, in the dog's month and pull it gently toward the back of the head.

A two-inch quill can disappear in a soft area of a dog in minutes, so speed is important. I have seen quills in a dog's leg muscle go in one side and within a half-hour come out the other. So the faster you remove the quills, the better. But if the dog does not cooperate, or you cannot do the job, get the dog to a vet as quickly as possible.

Sometimes we forget about the small things that make a dog perform better, or feel more comfortable. For example, to beat the heat, immerse your dog in cool water when available. While in the field, always carry water if you think it is not available in the area. As long as you and your dog have water, you'll both have more energy. Carry a dog biscuit or two in your hunting vest as well.

I don't leave the field when a porcupine strikes. Instead, I extract the quills as quickly as possible.

Sore or cut feet take the pleasure out of hunting for you and your dog. Foot protection is as important for your dog as it is for you. What leather boots with Vibram soles do for you, pads do for your dog. But while boot soles are an inch thick, a dog's pad is only a fraction of that. This means that rocks, sand burrs, cactus, frozen ground, and rocky slopes can cut, or wear down a dog's pads quickly. For every mile you walk, add ten for your dog. Preconditioning is the best way to prevent sore feet, which means getting dogs out to exercise regularly long before the hunting season begins. You'll be amazed how quickly a dog can toughen up its pads over a period of days. Pad-toughening compounds can be extremely helpful in maintaining a dog's pads as well. If a dog does cut or wear its pads down it's essential to administer healing compounds after the hunt, and continue with it until they heal. At times, dog boots may be necessary, and the prep work is well worth it.

A hard-working dog can also wear the hair and skin off its underparts quickly. Buckbrush, rose bushes, stubble fields, prickly pear cactus, and sharp rocks all wreak havoc on a dog's belly. If a dog shows signs of redness on its belly after the hunt I apply baby oil or Bag Balm. Tummy protectors also can be quite useful when hunting in some areas.

Burrs are not a serious threat, but can be uncomfortable, especially under legs, and around ears and eyes. Carry a small comb to free the burrs, and take the time to check your dogs regularly.

PLANNING A TRIP

Planning an upland bird hunting trip is not like planning other vacations, because birds are not in fixed locations. Populations change from year to year. This is why spur-of-the-moment hunting trips to unfamiliar places are usually doomed to fail unless you have a contact that gives you information on a daily basis. For instance, I received a call one day from a guy in North Carolina asking about hunting gray partridge in Montana. My first question was, "When are you planning on coming?"

There was a long pause. "In about a week," he said. "Years ago, a friend of mine hunted big game along the Missouri Breaks over Thanksgiving weekend, and saw lots of partridge on the way to the hunting camp. I was planning on flying commercial, renting a hunting rig big enough to carry a couple of pointers, and hunting five or six days."

This time there was a long pause on my end. "Let me get this straight," I said. "You had a friend who hunted the Breaks years ago, and you plan to come out here on the thirtieth of November, right? Let me put it this way. For the past several years our autumns have been mild, with little snow. In fact, the last four years I've hunted for upland game birds just about every day right up to the last day in December, and it has been fairly dry. I'm not telling you not to come this year, but if you do, bring cross-country skis or snowshoes. This year, most of the state is covered with ice and wind-driven snow. I don't think your pointers will be much help. If you are after Huns with pointing dogs, you may be out of luck. I'm not saying you won't find birds, but with the drifting snow we have, the backcountry roads are closed."

Montana's upland bird hunting season lasts over one hundred days, starting September 1, and ending January 1. If I miss a day in the field in Montana it's usually due to traveling to other states to hunt, or because of bad weather here. Most years, snow usually arrives before Thanksgiving, with continuous cold fronts moving across the northern plains. High winds sometimes follow the storms, crusting the snow and flattening vegetation, making it impossible to hunt effectively. Game birds become highly visible and wary, making approaching them next to impossible. The point is, you have to check the weather. Don't assume autumn weather will be the same year after year.

A planned hunting trip can also be doomed if you ignore reports from individuals or agencies with local knowledge. Years ago a friend and I had talked about hunting prairie chickens. Both of us had hunted them before, but never in the place we were planning to go this time around. The year before there was a banner crop of both sharp-tailed grouse and prairie chickens. The mixed prairie grasslands had adequate moisture, and bird numbers on the leks had increased. Carryover cover for nesting looked promising as well.

Our plans were stalled for a year, but the following season was a go. In early spring I made a phone call, and talked to a wildlife biologist friend about bird numbers on the leks. The information I received was not good. I called back in late summer, and the reports were not any brighter.

We had plenty of dogs, and neither of us was interested in shooting a large number of birds. So instead of looking elsewhere, we decided to hunt the grasslands as planned. After three hard days of hunting thousands of acres, alternating dogs every two hours, and only finding a few sharptails and no chickens, we called it quits. After that first day of unsuccessful hunting, we should have moved on.

My next trip was outstanding—I actually listened to what the local folks had to say.

Trips should be planned for a specific area, but no more than nine months in advance. Three months is better because you can take advantage of reports on population densities during breeding season and recent brood counts. I plan hunting trips every year. One reason is to extend my hunting season; the other is to hunt different species of upland game birds not available in my home state.

Weather is the most unpredictable factor in planning a hunting trip, but seasonal weather reports from previous years can be helpful if kept in perspective. If you encounter foul weather, and it is not widespread, you might consider an alternate location close by to make the hunt a success.

NEW HUNTING DESTINATIONS

This is my plan of attack when I travel to a new upland bird hunting destination:

1. I decide what species I'm going to hunt. I then research the birds—habits, habitat, and the best way to hunt them. I study distribution maps to see where the greatest concentrations of birds have been in past years.

2. I select two or three locations. I research the Internet and make phone calls directly to the federal and state agencies involved with land use and hunting: U.S. Department of the Interior, Fish & Wildlife Service, national wildlife refuges, national forests, national grasslands, Bureau of Land Management, state fish and game departments, Indian reservation agencies, state wildlife refuges, state departments of tourism, and individual fish and game wildlife managers. Then I check locally: chambers of commerce (chamber people often are helpful in providing names of local people with information), sporting goods stores, motels, veterinarians, outdoor newspaper reporters, librarians, hunting books, guidebooks, magazines, and other local articles and publications.

3. I select the final area and concentrate on local information.

4. I pick an alternate location as a backup, in case bird populations have declined. Go where the birds are, not where they used to be.

5. As the trip draws near, last-minute reports are essential. I call the most reliable contacts for the latest information on populations and weather conditions. Be prepared to change plans if need be.

6. I set dates to coincide with the most favorable weather conditions in that region and the early hunting seasons, but not necessarily opening day.

I also recommend consulting my *Wingshooting Wisdom Guide Series*, published by Willow Creek Press. The second part of each guidebook includes extensive details on how to plan a successful bird hunting trip. The idea for this book series came to me on two fronts. After many years of hunting across North America, I realized that no helpful step-by-step guide existed for hunters interested in locating and hunting a single game bird. And as an avid bird hunter, photographer, author, and columnist for *Pointing Dog Journal*, I had received hundreds of inquiries from traveling wingshooters who wanted help in zeroing in on birds in unfamiliar country.

FROM FIELD TO TABLE

Prairie game birds can be the most delicious of upland birds, or as dry and dull as last week's leftovers. Young birds shot early in the season will be delicate, and can be cooked the same day for lunch or dinner. While old-time market hunters said the sooner cooked after killing the better, I believe hanging the birds will make them even more tender. A good upland game bird meal begins with the pull of the trigger, because lack of proper field care can ruin dinner. In warm weather, I field draw and wash out the body cavity with cold water, and then hang the bird, or place it in a cooler with ice. I hang my birds for several days, then pick, skin, or fillet the breast (saving the legs), depending upon how I am going to prepare them for the table. Game birds that have been properly field dressed and cared for are easy to cook.

I often use the same recipes for dark meat and light meat, although the cooking times may vary. Prairie chicken, sharptails, and sage hens all have dark meat. Young Huns, pheasant, ruffed grouse, blue grouse, and spruce grouse are all fairly light meat, but when mature they become a bit darker in color.

I believe young ruffed grouse are the most tender and delicate of all the upland game birds. They can be picked or skinned. The breast and legs are white meat, and can be prepared in as many ways as tender young fowl. At the other end of the scale is the sage grouse, with very dark meat; the rest of the upland game birds fall in between.

People have differing opinions about eating sage grouse. Some find only young birds taken in early season palatable, while others think all sage hens taste bitter. I think they are delicious if properly prepared, and it is particularly important to field dress these large birds as soon as possible after shooting. I usually fillet the breast, and cut the legs into pieces.

If you have an old bird, don't attempt to prepare it as you would a young one. Older game birds can be leaner, with darker and drier meat, and should be cooked in sauce or with olive oil and butter. Don't cook wild birds like domestic chicken. They should not be overcooked, and are best when still pink inside. To help keep the meat moist, soak it in milk or marinate it for several hours before cooking.

Tailgate cooking is a good way for the traveling wingshooters to enjoy the fruit of their labor.

TAILGATE COOKING

Tailgate cooking is a good way for traveling wingshooters to enjoy the fruits of their labor. When done right, it is fast, easy, and economical. One only has to make a simple traveling cook kit to have the meal of a lifetime. House all the essentials in one container: small portable cook stove, Teflon frying pan, sharp knife, scissors, dishes and utensils, clean-up supplies, plus the ingredients for the recipes you are going to make.

Here are some of my favorite quick and easy recipes, but be sure to try your own. Serve recipes with hard rolls and a green salad. Good luck, that's all there is to it.

BEN'S TAILGATE HUNS

Skinned Hun breasts and legs (or any filleted game bird breast)
Milk to cover birds
Olive oil and butter
1/2 cup bourbon or water
1 cup sour cream
Salt and pepper to taste

Soak breasts and legs in milk for three to four hours. Dry and fry quickly to sear in equal parts of butter and olive oil (insides should remain pink). Remove birds and lower heat. Add 1/2 cup bourbon or water and the sour cream. Simmer briefly. Salt and pepper to taste. Serve sauce over birds.

ANOTHER GOOD SAUCE

1 cup peach or apricot preserves or orange marmalade
1/2 can of beer
2 tbsp butter

Heat until boiling. Serve over birds.

GRILLED TAILGATE GROUSE

2 or 3 cut-up grouse (or any game bird)
1/3 cup tamari or soy sauce
Juice of one lemon
1/4 cup oil

Mix well, and put in plastic bag in the cooler before you leave to go hunting. Drain and grill when you return.

TAILGATE PHEASANT IN BEER BATTER

3/4 cup beer
1 cup pancake mix or white flour
Cooking oil
Salt and pepper to taste
Filled breast chunks and leg parts (or any filleted game bird)

Mix beer and pancake mix or white flour to form batter. Dunk chunks of meat and drop into hot oil. Be careful, as the meat cooks quickly. You can also substitute Shake 'N Bake for the batter mix.

IN THE KITCHEN

Here are a few of my favorite recipes for when you're back at home in your own kitchen after a successful trip.

GAME BIRD CACCIATORE

Breasts and legs from two or three birds
One chopped onion
Olive oil to cover the bottom of pan
One can Italian-style stewed tomatoes
1/2 cup white wine or chicken broth
Salt and pepper to taste
Cooked pasta

Heat olive oil in a large skillet or iron pan. Add birds and brown on both sides until pink. Remove birds and brown onions. Add tomatoes, wine or chicken broth, and salt and pepper. Cook until the sauce boils, and then simmer for five minutes. Add cooked birds and serve over pasta.

HUNS IN SOUR CREAM

    Breasts and legs from several Huns (or any game bird)
    One pint sour cream
    One can cream of mushroom soup
    One can mushrooms
    Salt, pepper, paprika
    3/4 stick of butter (6 tbsp)
    Cook Huns in water until tender (save water). Remove meat from bones. Mix remaining ingredients together, add Huns, and put in a 9-by-12-inch greased glass pan. Mix 1 cup water saved from Huns and butter. Heat until butter melts; cool and pour over 1 small pkg. Pepperidge Farm Herb dressing. Mix well and place on top of sour cream–Hun mixture and bake at 350 degrees for 45 minutes.

BEN'S HUNS IN CHAMPAGNE SAUCE

    6 Huns (or pheasant or mountain grouse parts)
    1 bottle champagne
    4 shallots, thinly sliced
    2 cloves crushed garlic
    4 tbsp ground juniper berries
    6 tbsp butter
    9 tbsp butter
    6 tbsp olive oil
    Marinate Huns in champagne, shallots, garlic, and juniper berries for at least one day. Reserve one-half cup of champagne. Sear quickly till just pink in the middle. Remove Huns and add reserved champagne. Boil champagne mixture and add butter, whisking to keep smooth. Pour over warm breast and serve immediately.

GLAZED BREAST OF GROUSE

Breasts of two grouse (or any light-meat game bird)

4 tbsp butter

1/2 cup currant or apple jelly

5 ounces dry sherry

salt, pepper, and paprika

4 tbsp heavy cream

Sear breast quickly in butter; add jelly and wine. Cook covered 15 minutes. Remove birds. Add cream, salt, pepper, and paprika and heat until it just begins to bubble. Pour sauce over meat.

BOBBIE'S HUNS AND MUSHROOMS

4 Hun breasts and legs (or filleted breast of any large game bird)

Flour seasoned with salt and pepper

Butter and olive oil

8 ounces mushrooms

8 ounces sour cream

1 can cream of mushroom soup

1 onion, chopped

1 cup dry white wine

Dredge Huns in seasoned flour and brown in butter and olive oil. Remove birds and brown onions in remaining oil. Add mushrooms; it may be necessary to add more oil. When mushrooms are browned, add white wine and simmer for a few minutes. Stir in mushroom soup and sour cream. Combine birds and sour cream–mushroom mixture and bake for 40 minutes at 350 degrees.

SAGE GROUSE WITH WINE

Sage grouse (or any dark game bird)

1 1/2 cup Burgundy wine

1 onion, sliced

1 bay leaf

1 garlic clove, crushed

4 whole cloves

1 tbsp brown sugar

Cut one or two sage grouse into serving pieces. Mix wine and remaining ingredients. Place pieces of grouse into a bowl or plastic bag. Add marinade, and let stand in refrigerator for 1-2 days. Remove birds and wipe dry. Dredge in seasoned flour and brown in hot oil. Strain marinade. Place birds and remaining liquid into a casserole dish and cover. Bake in 300-degree oven for 1 to 1 1/2 hours.

SKILLET GROUSE

3 to 4 young prairie grouse

Milk to cover

1/2 cup whole wheat flour

1/2 tsp salt

1/4 tsp pepper

1/2 tsp thyme

4 juniper berries, crushed

1/4 cup olive oil

Sauce

3 tbsp butter

1 tbsp flour

1 cup of milk

Salt and pepper to taste

2 tbsp sherry wine

6 pieces of toast spread with currant jelly

Cut down the side of backbone and remove. Cut down both

sides of the backbone "T" with game shears and remove part of the ribs. Cut bird down the breastbone. Place halves in bowl and cover with milk. Set aside for at least an hour. Combine whole wheat flour, salt, pepper, thyme, and crushed juniper berries. Remove grouse from milk and roll in flour mixture. Brown both sides in the olive oil, 20 minutes or less. While birds are cooking, prepare sauce and spread toast with currant jelly. Melt 3 tbsp butter in small saucepan. Stir in flour, cooking slowly. Gradually add milk, salt, pepper, and sherry wine. Place grouse on toast and pour sauce over birds.

SUMMER GROUSE SALAD
　　1 cup uncooked wild rice
　　2 cups diced cooked grouse (any game bird)
　　2 tbsp seasoned salt
　　1 cup green grapes
　　1 cup sliced water chestnuts
　　1 cup mayonnaise
　　1 cup cashews

Prepare wild rice according to package directions. Drain and cool. In a large bowl, mix mayonnaise and seasoned salt. Add wild rice, grouse, grapes, and water chestnuts. Cover and chill. Just before serving, add cashews. Serve on a lettuce leaf.

SIDE DISHES

BEN'S FAVORITE BRAISED CELERY

4 cups sliced celery or chard
1 tsp fennel powder
4 tbsp olive oil
1 tsp basil
2 tbsp butter
Salt and pepper to taste
1 tsp dry mustard
Cream

Cut celery into 1-inch pieces. Place all ingredients except cream and mustard in heavy skillet. Put in 400-degree oven and bake for 10 minutes; reduce heat to 350 degrees and cook 12 minutes more. Spoon celery into serving dish. Add cream and mustard to skillet. Heat and pour over celery.

WATERCRESS SALAD

Watercress
1/2 cup crumbled blue cheese
2 pears; seeded, cored, and cut in quarters (canned pear halves can be used)
2 tbsp red wine vinegar
Juice of half a lemon
1/2 cup olive oil
Salt and pepper to taste
1 tbsp heavy cream

Mix vinegar, oil, lemon juice, cream, salt, and pepper. Toss with watercress. Put pears and blue cheese on bed of watercress.

WILD RICE

1 cup wild rice
4 tbsp butter
4 slices chopped bacon
1 small chopped onion
1/2 cup diced celery
1 small can mushrooms
1 tsp seasoned salt

Prepare rice according to package directions. Fry bacon until crisp. Sauté celery and onions in butter. Add mushrooms and seasoning. Mix with wild rice.

FIELD NOTES

FIELD NOTES

FIELD NOTES

FIELD NOTES